SHATTER
SOME
WORLDS

Reinventing, Realizing, Reintegrating

SHATTER SOME WORLDS

Reinventing, Realizing, Reintegrating

ANDREW S. TIRADO

ARPress
ILLUMINATING IDEAS.
EMPOWERING VOICES

ARPress
45 Dan Road Suite 5
Canton MA 02021

Hotline: 1(888) 821-0229
Fax: 1(508) 545-7580

Ordering Information:
Quantity sales. Special discounts are available on quantity purchases by corporations, associations, and others. For details, contact the publisher at the address above.

Printed in the United States of America.

ISBN-13:   Softcover   979-8-89330-734-4
           eBook   979-8-89330-735-1

Library of Congress Control Number: 2024902804

CONTENTS

PREFACE

This year, 2022, I, Andrew Scott Tirado, am republishing my earlier publication entitled- Shatter Some Worlds: Tales of Professional Liars and Those of Us Who Say, "Hey, you're Full of Shit". Back in 2006, when I first published I had a particular publisher that I worked with on the project. Now this year, I am working with a new and different publisher. The content of my book is now being offered to potentially a new audience and will hopefully be getting the right kind of exposure. With its new alterations & tweaks, my book will likely have better lucrative success.

After my writing was first published, I've encountered some notable milestones that I'd like to mention here. Firstly I'd like to state and have the included image in this book serve as proof that I graduated from Florida Gulf Coast University's College of Business with a bachelor's of Science degree concentrating in Entrepreneurship in 2009. Unfortunately, my second notable mention that I'd like to include here is the premature passing of my father at the age of 49 from terminal cancer, which also happened in 2009. For the next seven years or so I had to learn to live without my dad who also lived for about seven years after his initial brain tumor diagnosis. By 2019, I had honed my own skill set enough to accomplish the third notable mention that I'd like to include here which happened to be my attainment of Florida statewide medical certification as a recovery peer specialist.

The certified recovery peer specialist (CRPS) designation qualifies me to serve four primary roles. They are: mentor, counselor, advocate, and change-agent all with regard to mental health care. The CRPS designation is one which an individual may be able to obtain through much "lived experience" as well as completion of certain scholastic/academic objectives. What one such as myself does with this designation can include assisting others with finding their own sense of recovery from substance use and/or abuse dependence, oversight for communities/populations of and with mental health conditions, attain employment with a recovery treatment facility or center, foster/

maintain/refine his or her own recovery including mental, physical, spiritual, emotional health outcomes, or even serve as a business proprietor or partner in the business of recovery healthcare.

Personally, I was led to and am proud to be a person in recovery who has the wherewithal to oversee my own recovery as well as assist others with possible navigation of their own functionalities. Through the years since I first published my book the feedback that I've gotten has somewhat centered around the term inspirational. When I set out to write my manuscript the intention was mainly to make a record of events as well as encompass a therapeutic experience for myself. Early on, after I published, the CRPS designation that was mentioned earlier really wasn't much of a thing, and definitely not here in Florida. I guess I've literally helped to expand the Certified Recovery Peer Specialist (CRPS) categorization locally, statewide as well as assisted with defining & refining the profession.

In conclusion, with regard to the original publication of my book from 2006, I need to offer some clarification. The manuscript was & is, much like my life, something of an artistic expression. Life is a coming together of art and science to a degree and that's definitely something that is exemplified in the writing. Trauma recovery, brain injury reintegration-the action or process of integrating someone back into society, dealing with post traumatic stressful situations, and successful functional adaptation to the rigors and challenges of the daily living of life can be quite scientific. I guess I would like to state that additionally my, my family's, and the community's efforts have really made the business of recovery a full-fledged part of the mainstream of society.

"Life's most persistent and urgent question is, 'What are you doing for others?"

Reverend Doctor Martin Luther King, Junior

"Live as if you were to die tomorrow. Learn as if you were to live forever."

Mahatma Gandhi

THE FLORIDA CERTIFICATION BOARD

HEREBY CERTIFIES THAT

Andrew Tirado

has met all the standards and qualifications of a certified
professional as determined and established by the Florida
Certification Board and is hereby conferred the title of

Certified Recovery Peer Specialist-Adult

CRPS100320-A
CERTIFICATE NUMBER

May 14, 2019
ORIGINAL CERTIFICATION DATE

CHAIRMAN OF THE BOARD

Florida Gulf Coast University

By virtue of the authority of the Board of Trustees
and on the recommendation of the University Faculty in the

Lutgert College of Business

has conferred upon

Andrew Tirado

the Degree of

Bachelor of Science

Management

With all the rights and privileges pertaining thereto.
Given at Ft. Myers, Florida this
Twenty-eighth day of April, Two thousand nine.

Provost

Chair, Board of Trustees

President

College Dean

Dedication

This book is dedicated to:

◊ **Jason Tirado**

◊ **Louie Tirado**

◊ **Ryan Tirado**

1

INITIAL

"Two things are infinite: the universe and human stupidity; and
I'm not sure about the universe."

—Albert Einstein

Started:

Friday, March 04, 2005

My life story begins in a tough, somewhat dilapidated, yet fully cultured old town called Brooklyn, NY. From what I can remember about being young, I had a pretty happy childhood, and my mom always brags that I as a baby barely ever cried, always kept myself occupied, and was very lovable. After living in New York until I was almost five years old, my family and I (two parents, and a younger brother who was two and a half years younger than me) moved to Cape Coral, Florida in April of 1984 when I was four, but almost five.

My parents wanted to get out of the "rat-race" environment of being in New York. They thought that Florida would be a better place for their kids to grow up. In their opinions Brooklyn was not a good place to raise kids. Well at least that's the story I've gotten, but I think I'm not getting the whole story.

The recollection of the first ten years of my life is mostly comprised of things that I've been informed of within the last decade or so. My father proceeded the rest of our family to Florida, and he traveled by car. After my dad had been here for about a year and established himself, my mother, I, and my younger brother flew down south to Florida on an airplane. Our parents had both come to Florida previously in the seventies before we were born.

When I was very young, my family and I lived on a street that had a fire station at the end of it. In the apartment located beside my apartment lived a little girl who was about the same age as me, and we use to play together. Her name was Jennifer. We were very young children, so we never really got close or anything like that. We were just childish playmates.

My family and I lived on Blake Court while we were in Brooklyn, which is in the part of town called Sheepshead Bay. I was kinda enjoying living in Brooklyn, but then we just suddenly moved to southwest Florida. I never got to know Jennifer because I was too young, so it wasn't really any problem for me coming to Fl. The transition wasn't difficult on me at all.

Since first coming to Florida, my life has taken some major unconventional shifts through time. Some of what life for me has been, is not totally unordinary, but sometimes it's difficult for me to believe that I've even survived this long. Every now and then I wonder why I've been able to turn out the way I have.

I started school after the first summer that I had been in Florida. My kindergarten year was spent at Gulf Elementary, and all I can recall from that year was my first experience with a wasp. That damn sucker bit me right on the arm and I thought I was going to die or at least my arm would fall off. For first grade, I went to a different elementary school called Pelican Elementary. In the first grade I think I had my first experience with kissing one of the girls that I went to school with. Second and third grades were pretty "run of the mill". I can remember at one time when I was in the fourth grade, I ran into a tree at P.E. because I was looking at my new sneakers as I was running.

At times during like second or third grade when I was at the bus stop after school, I'd end up getting into a fist fight with one of the other neighborhood kids named Charlie. The fights with Charlie were never too serious. They were more less expressions of two young kids just being violent for no good reason. I think we ended up gaining some kind of respect for each other through the fights.

There was another neighborhood kid named Michael who I'd also get into fights with, but he didn't go to my bus stop. I guess it was around the same time- frame that I would get into fights with Charlie that I'd fight with Michael. Michael would never beat me in a fight, but he always kept tryin'. We'd fight after school too, but it was always later in the afternoon/evening when our confrontations would occur.

I stayed at Pelican through the fourth grade but didn't end up completing elementary school there. The reasoning for my not completing elementary school at Pelican was really because of the first of those major unconventional events of which I mentioned. I'll get to the full explanation of that in a bit.

Between the ages of five and ten, I was always competing in athletics in what- ever way possible. During my years in elementary school, I was considered to be one of, probably the fastest runner at my school. At P.E. and/or recess I may have been looked at as the all-star athlete. On one occasion, when I was at P.E., I completed the mile run in less than six minutes. One of my other key athletic accomplishments was that I made the highly selective, precision jump rope team at Pelican.

BMX—Bike racing started for me when I was about seven or eight and I'd constantly take-home blue ribbons. The funny thing about it was that most of the kids who I was racing against had these expensive bikes and outfits, but I just rode a cheap non-specialized bike and wasn't worried about my outfit either (just wore a helmet along with comfortable clothes). I stopped racing after I wrecked pretty badly on the track one day (the first big risk I can remember taking), and my parents just told me, that's it; you're not doing that anymore". There weren't any serious injuries though.

That ended my stint with bike racing as an organized sport. I continued riding my bike though. There are about three other times that I can recall where I almost severely injured myself from bicycling before the age of ten.

Once, when I was at the park with some friends, and we were all jumping a ramp just to see how high or far we could go. When my turn came up, I rode my bike up to the top of a large hill to gain speed and a bunch of momentum. I rode down the hill, hit the ramp (which was a piece of wood that was set up against a concrete slab at a 45-degree angle with the ground), and went much farther than I expected to right into a sturdy wooden table that didn't budge after I collided with it. Ouch!

As a condominium was being built, there was a large pile of dirt placed near the end of the parking lot. I decided that I should use the dirt mound as a ramp and try to do some cool kind of trick from it. With an audience of neighborhood friends watching, I rode down to the opposite end of the parking lot from where the mound was and started gaining all the speed I could. I hit the dirt mound with all my speed and ended up in a palm tree in my friend's yard which was adjacent to the condo construction site. That was definitely not a cool trick.

On another occasion a friend of mine and me were riding down a somewhat commercial street in the bike lane. I was riding a little bit ahead of my friend. As we were riding, a large dump truck was approaching us from behind traveling moderately quickly. Just before the large truck passed us, my friend sped up alongside of me, and jumped from his bike and tackled me to the ground. At first, I got kind of mad, and said, "What was that for?" He told me that if he hadn't done that then we both would have been sucked under the wheels of the dump truck due to the suction from the speed of the truck, and how close it was to us.

2

LOCATED

"A coward dies a thousand deaths; a soldier dies but once."

—Anonymous

Between fifteen and twenty years later–

Currently I am in my junior year at Florida Gulf Coast University in Ft. Myers, FL. The degree that I will attain will be a B.S. (Bachelor of Science) in Management through their College of Business. I've been studying business administration and management for about seven years now. After I graduated from high school in June of 1997, I decided to attend vocational school instead of entering college or the workforce immediately. I wasn't sure if I wanted to go to college, and my grade point average was pretty low, so I was advised to try vocational school.

I had no prior work experience, but near the end of my high school years I was doing a lot of drawing. Mostly what I drew was comic book characters, but all the other amateur artists seemed so much more talented than me, so I didn't want to pursue it. Architectural Drafting was one of the programs that the vocational school offered, and that seemed like something that might work out for me. After being in the drafting program for nine weeks I was failing to grasp the necessary basic skills required. So, I decided to try something else, which happened to be their Business Administration program.

That program worked out for me. I completed the year and a half program in July of 1998. Once I graduated from the vocational school, I entered the employment market. I was hired at a local telemarketing company. That only lasted for about five months because I decided to start at a local community college called Edison Community College. I suppose I could have kept my job at the telemarketing company, but most of my reasoning for wanting to start at Edison was because I didn't want to be a telemarketer for the rest of my life.

I started at Edison Community College in January of 1999, which happened to be the spring semester. By the fall semester I was working for the Public Safety department on campus as an office assistant. A few months prior to starting at the Public Safety office I was employed with another telemarketing company which only lasted for two months. That telemarketing stuff is easy to get a job at, but it just wasn't for me.

My employment in the Public Safety office lasted just over a year and a half. I was told that my services were no longer needed due to downsizing, so I went to look for a job off campus. I really felt like their reasoning for terminating me was more discriminatory than anything else, but I never pursued that angle. That experience left a bad taste in my mouth, so I didn't want to look for further on- campus employment at that time. There began my ten-month job hunt.

During the first few months I collected unemployment while I was looking for a new job. After unemployment paid me for the number of weeks, they deemed me to be entitled to, they sent me a letter telling me that they had made a mistake, and that I needed to send back all the money they sent me. Yeah right, all that money had been spent, and I had no job so how was I supposed to pay it back. I didn't feel like they were entitled to it back anyway. My job hunt continued.

It was getting tiring going on the job search daily, and constantly being rejected, but I kept on. Day after day, week after week, month after month I filled out applications, and went on interviews at the same time as I was enrolled in classes at Edison. One morning when I was on my way to school, I was talking to someone about my situation, and he advised me to write a letter to the editor at a local newspaper. So, I did it, and the letter ended up being printed. I still didn't get the satisfaction I was after though.

In April of 2002, I finally went back to look for an on-campus position. After I had a meeting with one of the VPs and the director of HR, we came a tentative solution. I ended up taking a position in the mailroom as a student-assistant/ casual labor helper.

By the time the Public Safety department laid me off I had already decided that I wanted to acquire a bachelor's degree from the newly formed University in town. The problem was that the Associate of Science degree that I'd be earning from Edison wasn't intended to be transferred into a bachelor's degree. The Associate of Science degree is intended for individuals who are planning on entering the workforce directly after earning it which I was not aware of. As a community college, Edison doesn't offer a bachelor's degree while Florida Gulf Coast University does.

While I was working in the Public Safety office as a student-assistant I some- times worked with other student-assistants. One student-assistant in particular and I became pretty good friends, and her name was Jenny. Jenny was in a long- term homosexual relationship when I first started working with her. She'd stayed in the relationship with her significant other for a total of I believe it was eight years, and I never really involved myself in any way outside of work with Jenny except for one time when I went to a party that her and her partner were throwing at their house. While Jenny was working at the Public Safety office at Edison Community College, she was also an undergraduate and then graduate student at Florida Gulf Coast University.

Jenny was pursuing the field of psychology, and she was always getting really good grades in it. Occasionally, Jenny would help me with a class assignment that I needed some assistance with. A couple of years ago Jenny had a big break-up with her partner, and shortly after that she stopped working at Edison. I heard she moved back up north because she was from Oklahoma, but I never heard from her again. I've tried to contact her through the internet but haven't had any luck so far.

I was faced with the dilemma of entering FGCU having certain credit for classes completed, and others not completed. If I'd stay at Edison and complete the classes that I'd need to earn an Associate in Arts degree, then I'd be able to enter FGCU as a junior and save a bunch of money by taking the same level classes at Edison. It would have been a stupid business decision on my part to enter FGCU without the AA degree from ECC. It took me between two and two and a half years to complete each of the Associate degrees, but it was a pretty good accomplishment for me considering the obstacles that I've had to overcome.

3

THE EARLY UNIT

"In order to form an immaculate member of a flock of sheep one must, above all, be a sheep."

—Albert Einstein

When my family and I first came to southwest Florida, my brother and I along with my parents frequently enjoyed spending time at the beach. As Jason, my brother, and I grew we'd stay close and do lots of things together. As a couple of kids, we were pretty much carefree. Once in a while we did get into fights, but usually it was with other kids. We learned many of life's youthful lessons together.

Jason was just very antagonistic. He'd push a person's buttons just for a cheap laugh, and he liked to make fun of people as well. He got on my nerves very easily, so I didn't really want him around me, and I tried to avoid him, but he always seemed to be around. If I'd go to a friend's place across town then he'd follow me over there. I'd try to ignore his antics, but that didn't work.

In Elementary School we, (Jason and I), were placed in the classes categorized for "gifted children". While we were smart, considered superior by our IQ's (in the mid-130 range I believe), our real passion was sports. We loved athletics (BMX racing, track and field, baseball, and football). Our favorite sport of all to play was basketball though. Video games, music and comedy shows were also of great interest to us.

Our parents were brought up under different religious faiths, and really came from different backgrounds by great measure. My father was raised with a strict Catholic upbringing, while my mother was raised under the Jewish faith. My parents didn't really shove down our throats, (like most parents do), religion. Through the years we did observe particular holidays, but I always saw things like that as being observed primarily for commercial reasons. Although I did appreciate to some extent, the traditional value of these events.

Two years after the arrival of our family to southwest Florida my second brother was born. My parents named him Ryan because at first, they thought they were having a girl baby, and the name Rosanna was picked out for the baby, but they didn't want to stray too far from the name they had agreed upon once they found the baby to be a boy. There was no way that they could name a boy Rosanna or anything resembling it. So, they just decided to go with Ryan for him.

Ryan was born with some complications (he came into the world with the umbilical cord wrapped around his neck, he was upside down, and he had a bowel movement during labor). Early in his life he was diagnosed with Attention Deficit Disorder (ADD), and use to take medication for it. Now he's nineteen, about six-two, and around two hundred and twenty pounds. He's not on any prescribed medication.

Our dad use to tell us (my brothers and I) how poor his family was when he was growing up, which caused him to drop out of school among many other hardships. There were times, he would tell us, when they had to live without electricity, and/or go hungry. My mom on the other hand, attended some college, and didn't grow up poor. My parents met when they were teenagers in Brooklyn, but they weren't quite the same economic class of people because my mom was pretty much well off.

When the family migrated to rural southwest Florida from urban New York City, my dad started working as a marine mechanic (building, fixing boats). At the first company he started at he stayed for about thirteen years, and I think managerial discrepancies were the reason for his leaving the company. That company was called Shamrock marine. My dad started at a very low-level position within the business, but by the time he left he had proven himself through his dedication, talents, and abilities to be a sought-after personality of the local industry. He took another job so that he'd be able to keep paying' the bills, but it didn't last long because it really wasn't what he was suited for.

After being out of the boating business for a couple of years my dad decided to go back to it. He started with Premium Parasail but ended up transferring over to Island Coast Boat Works. My dad was working for Island Coast for a few years when he started having these spells (auras) overcome him and he would occasion- ally pass out for a few seconds while on the job. Luckily no damage or injury ever resulted to the company or any of its employees or my dad from my father's mysterious illness.

Dad and his co-workers became very concerned, so my father entered one of the hospitals in town to find out just what was going on. The doctors instructed him to take a magnetic resonance imaging

(MRI) test. The MRI test revealed that my dad had a brain tumor. The type of tumor that he had was a cancer that surfaces in children, but my dad was forty-two years old, so this didn't make sense.

At this hospital here in Fort Myers (which is right outside of Cape Coral), they told my dad and his family and friends that he only had about six months to live, and that he needed to get his affairs in order. Shortly thereafter dad checked himself out of there. Dad's entire life started imploding all around him. Almost everything that he had become accustomed to was no longer applicable.

Initially, my father returned home from the hospital, and started doing some pretty nutty things (doing non-prescribed drugs, not taking the prescribed meds, excessively drinking, staying out for days on end). Violence between my parents went on, and my mom had to take out a restraining order on him. After that happened between my parents, my dad traveled all the way up the east coast to stay with his sister in Staten Island, NY, where the Staten Island University Hospital is located. At the hospital the doctors utilized laser radiation treatment along with medication successfully, and his cancer went into "in remission". While my dad was being treated at the Staten Island University Hospital, my parents did communicate enough to decide to try to live together again, and not get a divorce.

Up until a short time ago I thought that when cancer is "in remission", what it meant was that it was cured. That's not the case though. What it means for cancer to be "in remission" is that the tumor or tumors are no longer growing. A per- son can still die when their cancer is "in remission".

By the time that my dad came back to Florida, my mom had moved into her own one-bedroom apartment. I had moved out of my parent's home by November of the year 2002, which was before my father had been diagnosed with cancer. When I decided to move out, I contacted a roommate service online. On the website, I listed my profile and other information. Shortly thereafter I was contacted by someone who had an extra room in his apartment that he was looking to rent out.

The next evening, I went to meet the guy who contacted me about the room- mate situation. We met in a public bookstore in town, and from there we went on to the apartment where I checked out the premises, got to know the guy some, and talked about money matters. A few days later I signed the lease and moved in. He asked me a question that I found a little peculiar to be asking of a person who just met him. He asked me if I had a girlfriend. I said yes, I do though, I said we're engaged and then told him about her a little.

We became pretty close friends. My new roommate and I would do things like play chess, watch movies, discuss political issues, order delivery food sometimes, and watch TV (sports, comedy shows, and crime dramas). When we'd watch Jeopardy, I'd have to tell him that I'm disqualifying you because you know too many of the correct responses. When I was rooming with Brian, I was working in the mailroom on campus, and taking classes at ECC.

4

RESPONSIBILITY

"A man's ethical behavior should be based effectually on sympathy, education, and social ties; no religious basis is necessary. Man would indeed be in a poor way if he had to be restrained by fear of punishment and hope of reward after death."

—Albert Einstein

My family life is quite extenuous. The immediate part of my family is just my parents and my brother. My father has four sisters, one brother, and both living parents; my mother has just one sister, but both of her parents are alive also. There are fourteen direct blood cousins that I have, numerous extended family members and lots of friends of the family. We're a closely knit group, but we don't take too kindly to one another's crappy behavior. Most things that go on in the family are fast paced, and we've always got to stay hangin' tough.

The Tirado side of my family could be regarded as a bunch of people who like to get loud on occasion and have a good time. Some of us could be considered party animals. On my mom's side, the family is more concerned with wealth and status, and therefore really more reserved. It seems that I don't know my mom's side of the family as well as I know my dad's side. Being preconcerned with greed makes people lose sight of things like family, and really other types of decency to an extent.

There's a good word "decency", let's see; I think that this capitalistic society that we live in is blurring people's impression of exactly what it means to be decent. In my little personal dictionary that I keep here in my desk, the word decent is described as better than mediocre but less than excellent. Decency is about more than that; if you ask me, it's about doing the right thing, and treating others respectfully. The problem is that our society has come to a point where respect has really been forgotten. My question is not whose responsibility it is to instill values in others(kids), but why the fuck have some people gotten them- selves involved in being parents when they really have no idea what they're doing.

Is it the responsibility of these musical artists or video game makers to teach kids values? No, that's pretty outlandish of a thought. These moron parents assume that responsibility when they bring new life into the world. I think I can see that I'm smarter in some ways than some people, but things like this just seem so obvious. Hello......films, TV shows, video games, music, and most books are forms of entertainment, and definitely not instructional methodologies.

Our entire mindset these days is kinda fucked. C'mon people, figure out that we've got to take responsibility for our own actions. Stop this damn blame game bullshit so these fucking lawyers can get each other rich off of the citizenry's stupidity. The other obvious problem to me is that we're too damn lazy. I guess convenience has come at a big price.

Parents have got to learn to make their kids take responsibility for their own individual actions, and not always be there to clean up their kids' messes (play the blame game). When the day finally comes when parents figure this out then we'll all be better off. Assuming responsibility for one's own actions is a basic principle that everyone needs to accept after a certain level of maturity. Its parent's responsibility to teach their kids right from wrong so if parents aren't willing or able to do this then they shouldn't have kids in the first place.

In some respects, laziness is definitely a choice, but it's another thing when establishment has made things so easy for people to do that they forget about what it means to expend effort. Now we're back to the money thing, there shouldn't be an elite top percent of the country that own a great deal of the money and occupy such a great amount of influence while people who were born into not so wealthy families suffer.

If the distribution of wealth was more evenly divided, then so many problems would be avoided. Homelessness and starvation for starters could be avoided. People do need to learn to depend on themselves to a point, but wealthy arrogant bastards shouldn't be controlling things while simultaneously squeezing out the middle class. "Assume responsibility for your own actions" has always pretty much been the way I've lived, and because of it I know that hard work and dedication can only take a person so far.

5

NEARLY FATAL

"The fear of death is the most unjustified of all fears, for there's no risk of accident for someone who's already dead."

—Albert Einstein

The year was 1989, and I was a fifth grader whose close friends lived across town from where I lived. My method of transportation at the time was mainly my bicycle. One evening in mid-September, I set out to make my way across town on my way home from a friend's house. Well, I didn't make it too far because when I got about five minutes away from my friend's house all hell broke loose.

As a ten-year-old kid with my carefree attitude, I was not well versed on the ways of the roadway. Anyway, I went out onto the median to cross the street and crossed out onto the side where oncoming traffic was approaching from. By the time I had fully crossed the median, a vehicle was right there to greet me. The problem was that neither I nor the driver saw each other because the water tower located in the center of the median was concealed by a great deal of shrubbery. The sports car was traveling at about thirty-five or forty miles per hour. The driver was an arrogant, old bastard from what I've been able to gather over the years because I've never been approached by him or anyone representing him outside of the court system at least.

The collision resulted in me and my bike shattering Mr. Mesh's windshield, and my bike and I being found about seventy-five feet away in a field. When I was first transferred to Cape Coral hospital my parents were told that I would probably not make it through the night. I had a collapsed lung, so I was on a respirator in addition to all the other machines that were being used to keep me alive. I guess after a short time in Cape Coral the doctors realized that I needed to go to another facility for further treatment.

I was airlifted to All Children's Hospital in St. Petersburg where doctors kept me in a drug induced coma to deal with my triple skull fracture. Doctor's per- formed a tracheotomy on me which left me with a device in my throat called a trake. The trake helped me breathe, but I suppose I found it to be rather annoying. I've been informed that I would take it out and throw it across the room.

While I was at All Children's Hospital, I had to wear splints (braces) on my hands and feet. I'd undo the Velcro on those and throw them across the room. Damn annoying shit. One of the doctors wanted to tie me down, but my dad told them no fucking way. As I was at All Children's Hospital, the doctors were keeping me in a drug induced coma in order for my body and brain to be able to deal with the massive head injury trauma because in a conscious state I imagine I wouldn't have been able to cope with the pain, and I would have just been overcome & died.

After a couple of months in St. Petersburg, I was transferred to Sarasota where I stayed at the Rehabilitation Institute of Sarasota. After a short time in Sarasota, I came out of my coma (weighing less than 60 lbs.). I had no idea what was going on, where I was, why I couldn't talk, why I was in a bed, or really even who the hell I was anymore.

At the rehab in Sarasota, where I stayed for six months, I kept pretty busy. As an inpatient at the hospital, physical, occupational, and speech therapies were a significant aspect of my daily life. Downtime was spent with the nursing staff, visiting family & friends, and other patients (inmates). I say inmates because the injured people who were there definitely didn't choose their fate and must have hated their situations as much as I did. It was sort of difficult to stay in a bad state of mind while there because everyone was so accommodating, and they seemed to have a way of making the patients forget that they were in a hospital which is part of the job of hospital staff's everywhere, so patients don't become overwhelmed with depression.

When I awoke from my comatose state, I realized that I had a device called a gasostromy tube implanted into my stomach. The device was pierced through the skin of my gut and went directly into my stomach. At mealtime the nurses would hook me up to a machine that would feed me a liquid meal, which I totally hated. They started feeding me ice chips, and eventually I moved on to eating cafeteria food.

I just had a really hard time keeping food in my stomach. Constantly, I was blowin' chunks (vomiting). Once in a while someone (family members) would sneak me some non-hospital food and I don't think I had much of a problem with any of that, but I definitely enjoyed it.

Damn that fucking hospital food though, that shit always made me throw- up. On a side note, I must mention that the phrase that started ringing in my head from the time that I awakened from my comatose state has been: "No pain, no gain".

Soon enough things became apparent to me. I had to relearn to do everything, and I don't mean just like walking and talking. I had to try to gain back my intellectual ability, learn to swallow and keep food down, balance and coordinate myself—which I still have a bit of a problem with, and generally just learn to adapt to the traumatic brain injury that I had sustained. I was definitely uneasy about the future, but I didn't think too much about that while I was in Sarasota.

Upon my arrival back home, I was in for much more adapting. Physical therapy continued all throughout my teenage years. Dealing with classmates was considerably rough for me because I had always been the guy that was able to do anything he wanted and everyone respected, ("Mr. Popular"). In middle school, as kids do, they made fun of me which really angered me. People who I considered to be my friends all treated me like some kind of freak, and that wasn't right. Through these tough times I did try to stay focused on my studies even though they were somewhat difficult for me too.

At first when I came home, I was using a wheelchair to get around. The wheel- chair didn't stay around for much more than a few months. When I started middle school, I was using a three wheeled walker, which I continued to use for about three or four years. In high school I started using a cane, and that I kept for a while, but ended up getting rid of that too. For now, and for the last seven years I've not been using any kind of brace to assist me with walking.

Since my traumatic brain injury (TBI), I've been informed of the reasoning behind the fact that I've been able to survive and maintain myself adequately well enough. The way I was before the car accident was superior mentally as well as physically, and because of it I've been able to recover the way I have been. I'll never be back to 100% of what I was, but I'm ok with that, and seriously after I look at what happened to me, I can't expect to be. I'm a man, who believes in science as an explanation for universal occurrences, but my second chance at life could be considered a miracle by some, and sometimes I feel that it very well could have been just that. Does God have a greater purpose for me?

My parents always made sure to tell me that all I needed to do was block out the unimportant crap that gets in my way, and just worry about concentrating on the things that I know are worth my time. Dad always made sure to tell me that I had to work on gaining the most amount of brainpower possible because I no longer was equipped with the physical capabilities that most people are able to depend on to compete. When my dad first started telling me that I didn't know what he meant, but through the years I definitely figured it out for myself. There have been many obstacles that I've had to learn to overcome through the years and the last few especially, but after it all, I really have to thank God for giving me such a great amount of resiliency-an ability to recover from or adjust easily to change or misfortune.

A lot of kids who come into the type of situation that I was in after my car accident just accept a life of dependency. I've really made it a point not to be like that. People, not all, but some try to make things more difficult for people with disabilities by telling them that they simply "just can't do it". The way that I've been dealing with that is by just bypassing those kinds of attitudes and proving myself capable. In the way I see it everyone requires some assistance sometimes, but when people do things for me, I always tell them that I appreciate it. "Don't expect and you won't be disappointed".

There was a lawsuit filed against the city of Cape Coral, against the parties who were responsible for building the water tower, and the driver of the vehicle. Nothing was achieved from the City of Cape Coral or the architectural group, but the vehicle's driver's insurance company did settle with my attorney's. I think it took about three or four years to finally become finalized, but it sure is a good thing that I've got the head on my shoulders that I do because if I wasn't able to go to school or hold a job then I'd just wither away and die with the amount of money that I was awarded.

Fear has always been a big hurdle for me to overcome; I mean after returning home after this catastrophic event which totally reshaped my life, I've had to accept a different kind of fear and learn to deal with it. My outlook on life dramatically shifted, but that definitely took some time. Really, I feel like I have to live in a constant state of reconfiguring things perpetually. Damn is that a pain in the ass, but I guess it kind of works that way for others too. Whatever, I don't give a shit.

Recently, and by that, I mean within the last few years, I've really realized that I've been kinda timid about stuff in the past. The thing is that fear is mostly just within a person's mind, and I don't really have much to be afraid of. Fear can really rule a person's life if they let it. I decided that the greatest fear that I had was death, and that death is just a natural process of the progression of life. So, I guess, the way that I see it is that I was pretty much born for dying.

6

TEENAGERS

"Education is what remains after one has forgotten everything, he has learned in school."

—Albert Einstein

It was 1992, in the fall, when I started high school totally feeling out of place. I knew some other students whom I had went to middle school with, but primarily high school was a foreign environment to me. During my freshman year I don't think I really did much hanging out with friends outside of school. There were a few friends that I did have though, and soon that few became a few more. There was this one girl who hung out with some of the people I knew, and I soon found out that she lived in the same neighborhood as I did.

So, during the ending part of my freshman year through the summer and into my sophomore year, I hung out with this chick a bunch. When I first started hanging' out with Kim, I was primarily listening to music like: Guns n Roses, Areosmith, light hip hop some, and Pop music. She was into heavy metal, and it rubbed off on me because I started listening to Metallica, Pantera, Offspring, Nine Inch Nails, Marilyn Manson and a whole bunch of other metal type music only. Our relationship was totally plutonic which was kind of strange in itself because at that time she had been considered to be the neighborhood slut.

This chick Kim was into some really hardcore metal stuff like black, death metal and even satanic shit, black leather, and chains. I never got into any of that satanic shit, and she never did any drugs because she was against that stuff. My brother, Jason never hung out with me and Kim because by that time he had his own things going on with his own group of friends, and he wasn't interested with tailing' me anymore. Kim wasn't one of the types of people he associated with anyway.

When I finished my sophomore year, and during the summer before my junior year, Jason and I met some other neighborhood kids who turned us on to some other, thuglier things. We started experimenting with drugs, and I had some really investigational times being what my best friend at the time called, "a goofy bastard". My nickname became Dru for a few reasons. Firstly, I was regarded as one of the realest and truest people in my neighborhood. Secondly, I liked to draw at that time. And thirdly, my full first name is Andrew so the Dru for short just worked.

Jason mostly hung out with Ben's younger brother Justin, at least at first. As some time went by Jason didn't really chill with anyone in particular but associated with lots of people. He developed lots of friends. Some of the individuals were just associates who he primarily had business dealings with.

My closest friend at the time (my ace), Ben, was a horribly bad kid. This guy had a considerable number of felony charges against him, made his way to and from correctional programs and juvie on a regular basis. We smoked (cigarettes, pot), drank (malt liquor, beer, wine, and hard liquor when we could), and tried to find girlfriends mostly. He was the one who would get into fights, sell drugs, do lots of stayin' hi, rob cars, and burglarize people's houses, ECT. I on the other hand, was just learning (tryin' to get some street smarts), trying to have fun, and get in where I fit in. That was sure a roller coaster of a learning experience.

Ben was from Tucson, Arizona. He had been a member of the street gang called The Cripps. His mom moved the family of Ben, Ben's brother Justin, their stepdad Bill, and herself across the country to Florida to try to get away from the gang life over there. But a person can't run away from their problems, they have to adapt to them and work to alleviate them. The thug life just followed them across the country, and kind of came to south Florida in sync with their arrival.

On one occasion early in our friendship, Ben and his "boy", John did some- thing to me that made me want to tear each of their heads off. The situation started by us getting a few quart bottles of malt liquor, and then going down a dock to drink 'em. The two of them drank their quarts real quick, jumped into the canal, swam to the other side, and then they started throwing mud at each other.

While they were assaulting each other with mud, I was sitting on the dock drinking my beer. I was amused by their antics, but after a short time they had had enough of the muddy canal dirt throwing. So, they swam back over to the dock where I was, and they pulled themselves out of the water.

Once they got onto the dock the two of them grabbed me and threw me in the canal. As soon as I resurfaced, they helped me back onto the dock. When I got back onto the dock completely, they threw me in again. Then they pulled me out again, and then threw me in again. That went on just like that, but eventually they quit. I'm not sure whether they just got tired of it or they saw how pissed off I was getting. By the time I had secured myself onto the dock I was ready to tear each of their heads off, but I figured that they weren't worth it so I just got the hell away from them.

I'm not really sure why I ever spoke to Ben again after that incident, but I guess it happens all the time (kids get into fights and then become good friends). I had only met the other guy, John once so he wasn't a friend of mine, and I only saw him once after that incident where I never said a word to him.

The gangs that developed over here were watered down versions of the real things that were in big cities. A bunch of people called the gangs in our area a bunch of wanna bees. I guess that's what they were because during the mid-nine- ties the thug life was in its early developmental stage.

Now, with the booming economy and population growth of this area things are different. Crime goes on in this area all the time, and the police are trying to keep it under control, but the criminal activity continues. For the first while that my family and I lived here in southwest Florida the area was pretty secluded. Within the last five or ten years though this area has become one of the fastest growing areas in the country, and I for one liked it better the way it was.

All of these people move down here from other parts of the country and bring all their money and development; well I think it was better before. That's evolution for ya, right? I say the local government should have set limits for the migration/development of this area, and still should now. The national government has some screwed-up system called the Immunization and Naturalization Service (INS), which is somewhat set up for that purpose. The INS needs to be modified and even overhauled and our local government needs to set up a population control program too.

On the first night that I went to chill with my thugged out pal, I almost had my head blown off by a large caliber handgun. It was totally dark out, and I went over to his place to meet him, but he had fallen asleep. I tried to wake him by tap- ping on the screen door, but his mom woke up first, and started questioning me in the dark, but I just blew her off. Then Ben woke up, and we just split. The next day I come to find out that his mom had a 45-magnum pointed at my head.

That night we went to see one of his "boys" (John) so we could get some pot (weed, grass, smoke, herb). The three of us smoked out and it was my first time, so I didn't really know what I was feeling, but it felt kinda good. After a while we smoked all the pot, and then Ben and I just left. That was that night.

I was fifteen when I met Ben who was fourteen, and at the time we hung out with lots of different people; he was a real people person. When we hung out, Tupac music was always around somewhere. I think he was one of the biggest Tupac fans I've ever met. This guy wasn't all bad though, he did take the wrap for me when we sent this other kid to the hospital one time. I've never been to jail, but that was about the closest I came.

One day during my junior year of high school (1995-96), I was hangin' out with this guy that I knew from middle school named Kenny (our moms were friends too), and Kenny called his girlfriend at the time, whose name was Ondreya, from a payphone. While they were talking, Kenny figured out that he had to go find a bathroom. When he left, he told me to talk to her until he got back, and I said sure. I don't remember what I said to her, but I remember get- ting the impression that she was very cold or in other words "totally bitchy". By the time he got back, I was relieved to be able to get off the phone already.

A couple of days later, I got a phone call from Kenny's girlfriend, and this time her attitude had changed. She told me that she had just called it off with Kenny, and I don't think the reasoning behind that was ever discussed. After talking to her for a while I figured that I wanted to call Kenny, so I got off the phone with her. I got in touch with Kenny, and I asked him if he minded if I started to get to know his ex. He told me that he didn't care.

As I started to get to know Ondreya over the phone, I realized that we should "hook-up", and she definitely seemed interested in getting to know me better. Unfortunately, Kenny wasn't ready to leave her alone yet. After about a week of us talking, she tells me that he comes over to her house late at night harassing her by knocking on her window, and she asks me if I can get him to leave her alone. I said, "Okay, I'll talk to him." So, I contacted Kenny, and told him to leave her alone.

He didn't listen, and Ondreya continued to tell me that he's still bothering her. This time when I contacted him I was pretty pissed off, and I threatened him. Even after I threatened him he still was doing his crap. I contrived with my closest friend at the time, Ben (who also knew Kenny), to have Kenny come over to hang out. When Kenny came over there wasn't any hangin' out to be had.

Ben lied to Kenny so he would come over by telling him that I wouldn't be there, and that we weren't really even friends. Stupid-ass Kenny believed him and showed up at Ben's place a little while later. As soon as Kenny saw me, he tried to run, but Ben wouldn't let him do that. For the next while I was yelling at Kenny trying to get myself really pissed off so I could just hit him. Unfortunately, Ben just wanted to fight this kid, so he got tired of me yelling at this guy real quick.

Ben said, out loud, "Aw, fuck that", and grabbed the weapon from my hand. Just as Ben said that Kenny started to run, but this time he was able to get away. As the two of them were running through the field, Ben just whacked Kenny on the back with the numb chucks. Kenny ran to an apartment where some people were home and called the cops. We immediately heard sirens.

We had nowhere to go so we just stood out in the street and waited for the police to show up. By the time they got there Ben had gotten rid of the weapon. Ben's brother was a guy who liked to talk, and I think he told the cops exactly what happened, but I think they had already been informed by other witnesses. Oh yea, Ben's brother, Justin, was outside with us too that day.

I recall standing out in the street with my hands in my pockets when the police showed up. For some reason I didn't take my hands out when the cops approached us. There were three officers, and one grabbed me by the back of the arms. He threw me on the hood of one of the police cars. He told me to never keep my hands in my pockets ever again.

I said I was sorry, and I wouldn't do it anymore. By that time the other officers had recovered the weapon. I was placed in the back of the police car along with Justin, and we had to fill out some paperwork. Ben had confessed to doing the deed, and the cops ended up taking him away that day.

In the end, Ben was the only one who actually was charged with any crime, and it was for assault with a deadly weapon. He was the only one who was charged because he was the one that actually used the weapon. I guess he told the cops that the weapon was his too. He must've also told the police that he was the one who instigated the fight. That was a pretty admirable thing of him to do, I think.

As for me, I carried on a long-term relationship with Ondreya. It wasn't long before the relationship became intimate. We spent countless hours on the phone and would spend time at each other's homes and would also meet at friends' houses. On Valentine's Day 1998, right after we went to see: "The Wedding Singer", I proposed to her. She happily accepted, but at age eighteen I wasn't really thinking clearly.

By the time I asked her to marry me, we had already had a few break-ups. When I proposed it was kind of a spur of the moment thing, so I didn't have a ring, and I told her that if we stay together without any breakups until your birthday (October 21), then I'll get you an engagement ring. We ended up breaking up in August, and from that point we learned that we weren't ready to pursue a marriage, but the relationship didn't totally come to a halt just yet.

Shortly after our break-up, my mom had found out that those individuals who'd had blood transfusions between certain times periods in the state of Florida were turning up with HIV positive blood. I'd had blood transfusions back in

1989 from my car accident, and I fit into the time frame for the state of Florida's proposed tainted blood. My mom highly encouraged me to go to the doctor's office and go get tested. After I explained my situation to the girl who I'd been intimate with regularly for the last while, she told me that she'd rather that I didn't get tested. She said that she'd rather not know, but if we are positive then we'll live and die together.

Her telling me that was very heartwarming and sweet, but I still had to know for myself. A short time later I went to the doctor's office, and had some blood drawn from my body. A couple of days later I had my results which turned out to be negative. While what my girlfriend told me was very pleasing, I did become concerned. If she had a response like that to a life-or-death situation like that then could she be hiding something from me? With the test coming out negative all was answered.

7

MISGIVING

"Great spirits have always found violent opposition from mediocrities. The latter cannot understand it when a man does not thoughtlessly submit to hereditary prejudices but honestly and courageously uses his intelligence."

—Albert Einstein

"A human being is part of a whole, called by us universe, a part limited in time and space. He experiences himself; his thoughts and feelings are something separated from the rest...a kind of optical delusion of his consciousness. This delusion is a kind of prison for us restricting us to our personal desires and to affection for a few persons nearest to us. Our task must be to free ourselves from this prison by widening our circle of compassion to embrace all living creatures and the whole of nature in its beauty."

—Albert Einstein

"Now he has departed from this strange world a little ahead of me. That means nothing. People like us, who believe in physics, know that the distinction between past, present, and future is only a persistent illusion."

—Albert Einstein

Jason and I were exposed to a whole new world of crime and adventure while we were hangin' out with Ben, Justin, and everyone else that we hung around with during the mid/latter-ninety's; we were livin' "Thug Life" baby. During summers throughout the 90's, Jason would go and spend time with family in New York. During those years my brother became very involved with a certain female named Nicole that he knew from his group of friends here in Florida. Nicole and Jason had a pretty chaotic relationship. Nicole was definitely what people would call a hottie back then (blonde, thin, model material, always with the "in" crowd, and always looking for a good time), and I think that was a big part of the problem.

While Jason was in New York he would always spend a bunch of his time with our uncle John. Uncle John is a big Italian guy who made lots of money not necessarily legally. Luxury cars, expensive clothing, extravagant hunting trips, and other high-priced goods and services were commonplace for our infamous uncle John. Jason became in awe of the lifestyle and grew to desire to emulate it.

The way I see it is that after my car accident Jason was left without a significant role model to aspire to be like which he had been used to. Early on he chose me to look up to, and then he decided that I wasn't worth looking up to anymore, so he chose his notorious uncle to try to be like. I'm not totally sure, but I think while Jason was in New York one of those summers he was even initiated into the "Latin Kings" street gang.

Jason and Nicole were never completely content with each other I don't think; to me it kinda seemed like a relationship that was for all the wrong reasons. They did have strong feelings for one another, but maybe it was less love than hate after a while. She really knew how to press his buttons (they we're always screaming at each other over the phone, and who knows what other kind of violent stuff they did in person). There were some serious mental issues that their illegal drug dependence may have eased temporarily, but in the end, it made things severely worse.

My brother, Jason, was always tailing me when we were young kids. That really got on my nerves at the time, I think. Then when I got into a car accident, and was gone for a while, I guess he really freaked out (I heard that he burnt down the field beside our house where our family was living at the time). When I came back home, he realized that he couldn't look up to me the way that he'd been used to anymore, and I think that left him somewhat lost. He saw what I had become, and in a way laughed at me at first, but then over the years assumed himself to be a great protector of mine.

When I was a sophomore in high school, I was enrolled in driver's education. Through the class I was able to acquire my learner's permit to drive a car, but when it came time to pass the road test in order to obtain a regular driver's license, I wasn't able to drive well enough. Shortly after my driver's education experience my brother decided to take me down to the DMV and see if I could take a road test there. When I was finally assisted, I found out that because of my disability I had to be approved by a person who has special certification through the state of Florida to approve persons with disabilities in order to acquire my driver's license.

Given this information, I started driving with an occupational therapist that had the state certification through a hospital in town. We drove for a few months, but I came to a point where I had stopped improving. I never acquired my driver's license then, and that was when I was about seventeen. All these years later I still don't have my driver's license because shortly after I was told that I'd stopped improving, and that I should come back in a few years, I lost my medical insurance.

A few months after I turned eighteen, Ben also turned eighteen. Ben, me, and another friend of ours all chipped in to buy a keg of beer and five cases of bottles of more beer for his birthday. We were planning on going out to the woods, having a bunch of people follow us out there, and just tryin' to have a good time drinkin' the night away. Ben, me, and Chris got all the booze and went back to Ben's place with it.

For some reason the police were already at one of Ben's neighbor's houses that night. Somehow Ben ended up getting into conversation with the cops who were there. The story of what was going on that night for us had been revealed, and the cop just told Ben to go ahead and have fun. So, we waited for my brother, Jason, and some other people to get there. The other carload of people arrived at Ben's place and shortly after we all just split.

The two carloads of us were on our way over to another person's place when the car that my brother was in got stopped for speeding. We all were right across the street from our destination, and our carload got pulled over too. I was in the back seat with the full keg of beer right between my legs, so all the cops had to do was point his flashlight in the car to look at me and he'd see the beer keg instantly. Sure, enough that's exactly what happened. The officer asked to see each of our ID's and found out that no one was twenty-one or over who was in the car.

By that time the police had swarmed around us. We had to take the keg out of the car and open the trunk. Opening the trunk revealed five more cases of beer bottles. The cops made the four of us stand out in the median and pour out each individual bottle. Damn, was I fucking mad that night.

The police confiscated our keg, and then took each of our names & other information to write us tickets with. The other three guys that I was in the car with were all on probation so that delayed the process even further and gave me more reason to be pissed. We were each written tickets and told that we had to appear in court on separate dates. They gave us tickets, humiliated us, and probably went and drank our keg, but on the positive side we didn't have to go to jail.

I think my ticket was in the amount of $175. That night I contributed $50 so the whole ordeal was good for one beer that ended up costing me $225. When I went to court, I pleaded no contest because I wanted to just put this ordeal behind me.

Unfortunately, that wasn't the last of my legal problems with alcohol as a minor. Not too long after that first incident, I decided to rent a hotel room so I could host a small shindig (party). My friend, Jason, was twenty-one so he bought the beverages. Besides my friend Jason and I, we had invited about five other people including my brother Jason. The small refrigerator in the hotel room was stocked to full capacity. When my brother came over, he brought over a few carloads of people.

Very shortly after my brother and his entourage arrived, there was a knock on the hotel room door. At the door was the police who told us that there were too many people in the room, and we needed to break up the gathering.

The officers told us that they needed to search the room for drugs, and we didn't know that we could have to them to go get a warrant, so we just let the illegal search happen. Having lots of people in a hotel room doesn't constitute probable cause. They found nothing illegal anywhere in the room until they looked inside the refrigerator and found all the alcohol. The police said, "none of you look over twenty-one so let's see some identification from each of you".

The cops checked all the ID's they could and found only one individual of age. My friend Jason received a ticket, the alcohol was confiscated, most every- body left, and that was the end of our party. Being the good guy that I am, I paid half of the ticket that Jason got that night. The friendship between Jason and I drifted apart a few months later though.

Jay, (my nickname for my brother), would do just about anything for me, but the way we were livin' in the lattter'90's was not the right way to be living. All the Mafioso movies, the rap (hip hop) music, and the dope game were where he chose to place his imagination along with his reality, and the mob bosses were who he looked up to. Films such as: "The Godfather" series, "Goodfellas"," Casino", "Scarface" as well as many others of the genre are the one's of which I'm referring, but he didn't just watch the movies he was living the lifestyle too (in the drug "dope" game).

My brother Jason was a big fan of DMX, Ja Rule, Tupac, Jay-Z, Notorious B.I.G., and Snoop Doggy Dog. He listened to a bunch of other stuff too, but it was all within the same type of music. He lived the music literally, which is something that I've learned over the years that you can't do. We really have to learn to use discretion better so we can decipher between things to take seriously and things not to.

For example, he started selling drugs. One Sunday evening when I was in my room, I saw Jason get dressed and run out with his girlfriend. About forty minutes later they came back. Jason's face and clothes were all bloody when he came into the house. He looked like he had just been jumped by group of people because his face was all bashed up, his clothes were all torn, and he was out of breath.

With busted lips, he said, "I just got my ass beat". I was in shock. I had never witnessed a scene like that before, and that was my brother. Then my parents came home, and they all left to go to the hospital.

I was pissed off at first, but then I found out that my brother had robbed these people for about $1500 in a drug deal gone badly. I wasn't going to involve myself and put my life in jeopardy because of something that I knew was wrong and criminalistic. This drug shit had gone far enough for me. From that point on

I really started hating the drug lifestyle and resenting people who lived it.

We were never rich growing up, but we always managed. Lots of people now- adays have no idea about hard monetary times, but others have it pretty bad, and we were always just in the middle. Jason and Nicole really divulged deeply into drug use, (marijuana, acid, mushrooms, ecstasy, ECT.), and my brother even became a dealer who came into a lot of quick money that was gone real quick. As the years went on, his debt and other bills and monetary obligations rose, his girl- friend problems got out of control, his family life drove him nutty, and drugs really became his only way out.

On November 30, 2001, just a couple of months after the terrorist attacks on the World Trade Centers, Jason took a fatal amount of drugs (at age twenty). He was scheduled to go to the Navy three days later, but instead, he had caused him- self to be brain-dead. What killed my brother, was it the fear of going to war, was it the craziness at home, was it an accident (something he didn't intend to do), or did someone kill him? Maybe it was a combination of all of these things or a couple, but all I know is that it was the most painful thing that my family and I ever went through (even worse than my car accident because I'm still here). At his funeral I really didn't know how to act, and I really just wanted to kill someone.

The substances that were found in his system were: alcohol, marijuana, zanex, and oxycontin. I believe that each of them had been consumed in excess amounts too. I guess that when a person starts taking pills to get hi, they've got to take more and more in order feel the desired effect until their body just can't take it anymore. Two months earlier he had asked me to take a drug test for him, and I just thought he was smoking some pot occasionally, so I did it for him. By that time, he was taking night classes at Edison too, so I thought he was trying to straighten his life up. I'm no detective and he was my brother, so I wanted to believe that he wanted to shape up.

About a year prior to his death, Jason had gone into my room while I was out and took a check out of my checkbook. He forged the check and brought it in to one of the branches of the bank that I use, and somehow got them to cash it. When I found out that he was responsible for doing that I got pissed. The first thing I did when I found out that the funds were missing was to find out from the bank where they went. The bank showed me a copy of the check, and after I told them that I did not sign or authorize that check they told me to go to the police and file a report. On the check was my brother's signature because when he presented the check to the teller, he/she made him sign the check before issuing him any funds.

The next time that I was able to, I filed a report about the theft. The police officer asked me if I wanted to press charges personally, and I said "yes". Immediately after I made the report, I called my mom to let her know about what was going on. I guess she let my dad know, and by the time I saw my dad that evening he was extremely pissed off at me. After arguing with him for a while, he ended up telling me that if I was going to be responsible for putting my brother in jail then I'd have to find a new place to live because I wouldn't be welcome with my own family anymore.

So, on the following day when I had a chance, I went down to the police station and dropped the charges. Eventually Jason did end up paying me back the money that he had taken from me, and somehow my mom was able to convince the bank not to charge him with bank fraud.

I regret not doing what I felt was necessary. Maybe if I did press charges on my brother he would have went to jail and learned some things the hard way. I wasn't ready to step up, be a man, and move out yet though. Who knows if pressing charges on him would have done anything positive anyway? I can't blame myself or my dad though (or can I?).

Ryan is doin' pretty good currently but dealing with Jason's death really affected him too. He was pretty devastated in the past, and he was only a mid-teenage kid when the death of his brother happened. Not that age helps a person deal with losing a twenty-year-old family member like I did when I was twenty- two. I think Ryan has been adjusting better lately due to the fact that he now has a steady girlfriend.

Fortunately, I had a steady lady of my own by the time my brother passed away who was really there for me for a couple of years after the ordeal. We had met in 1999, when I first started going to Edison Community College, and her name was Christine. She was a little older than me, and unfortunately, she was strickened with cerebral palsy. When we first met, she really didn't have much of a problem with being physically disabled as well as mentally because she was classified as bipolar. Bipolar means having a manic, depressive personality and cerebral palsy is a neuro-muscular ailment acquired at birth which affects body movement, speech, hearing, and other necessary life functions.

We really fell deeply in love with each other despite each other's shortcomings. In my mind we would be together forever, and we even talked about dying together so neither of us would have to go on without each other. After a year and a half of dating, we became engaged, but becoming a family with a baby was really met with a huge amount of opposition especially from her family. Christine was a young lady of great taste and style. She had a financial wealth of her own, and loved spending money on things like jewelry, make-up, pedicures, hair styles, gift giving, doctor visits, medicines and restaurants. My lovely Christy was one of the greatest teachers I've ever had in my life, yet her IQ was minimally less than average (around 90). People who we choose to keep as our closest friends usually end up teaching us many things through involved life experiences, but she was "something else", whew.

Christy and I carried on a four-year relationship outside of school. We would see each other at school and talk to each other for about two years before we started calling each other a couple. We really developed quite a connection that a lot of people in significant other relationship strive to acquire but have a difficult time attaining. At times though we'd each do and say things that we'd need to explain to the other, but that's pretty normal to an extent. There's got to come a time when the two people in our type of relationship reach a point where they've got to be free to do what they want, but at the same time try to keep the other person happy.

When Jason passed away, I got a phone call from Ben, because at that time he was living in Kansas doing God knows what. I told him that I wasn't into the kind of stuff that we'd been involved with in the past (drugs, gang stuff, getting arrested, or generally running wild). I also told him that if he was still into that stuff then not to come around me because I was trying to leave that crap behind and concentrate on my career and my mew lady. I never heard from Ben again.

I also never made any effort to keep in touch with any of the other people that Jason and I hung out with when we were teenagers. Once in a while I'll see some- one from our old crowd in public, who we use to know, and I'll say hey and maybe do some small talk, but that's about it.

Approximately eight months into our relationship Christy and I became pregnant. Some guys don't see things like that as a we think, but I surely did. That surprised Christine which I didn't quite understand at first. We decided to go through an abortion. I ended up taking her to the #1 (top rated) gynecologist in town. From that point I made sure to accompany her on her visits on every occasion that I could.

For some ignorant reasons, neither of us thought that we would get pregnant. We certainly did though. While we were going to the doctor's office, we were trying to keep what was going on kinda quiet. She didn't want her mom or the rest of her family to know about it. That went over for awhile but eventually her mom found out.

The evening that we had actually done the abortion we spent the night together at my parents' place. My mom was being morally supportive of the situation, and really just cool about the whole ordeal. Christy had not spent the night with me prior to this. At about 4am her mom comes over to my parents' place and starts ringing the doorbell. I got up and answered the door.

She knew that Christy was spending the night with me, and she didn't approve of that (even though Christine was almost twenty-four years old at the time). She had me go get her daughter so they could leave. I should have told her to go home, and Christy will be back in a while, but I went back to my room where Christine was and informed her that her mom was there to pick her up. Shortly after that they just left.

It was 4am, and I had been startled awake by the doorbell. A person can't think straight under those conditions. Christine's mother wouldn't have listened to me anyway. I really wasn't into a fight with her or at that time of the morning with anyone. Damn her, I just wished she could have left Christy and me alone.

I guess that after they left my place that morning Christy ended up confessing to her mom just what was going on. I'm sure that her mom told her that she didn't want her to see me anymore. Oh well, that didn't happen. We still remained a couple and made it a point not to let her mom dictate our relation- ship. That was definitely tested by events yet to come at that point in our relationship.

We continued to make love after the abortion. Her gynecologist prescribed birth control in the form of the pill for her which she took regularly. I knew that Christy was taking some other prescription meds, and I really wanted to limit the amount of foreign substances she was putting into her body. I came up with a couple of suggestions. Neither of them ended up panning out.

The first thing that I thought of was to look into male birth control, but we decided against that. The other thing that I suggested doing was pretty shocking. I told her that I could get a vasectomy. She told me that I was crazy, and that if I ever did that she would leave me. We knew we wanted a baby, but I suggested adoption when we were both ready.

The adoption thing wasn't out of the question for her, but she really wanted to give birth to my child. No woman should ever be told that she can't do that have someone's baby, but certain members of her family did tell her that anyway. We even discussed it with our gynecologist, and he told us that lots of women with CP have successful births so we shouldn't be frightened to go through with it. A huge concern of both of ours besides the labor process was the fact that she was on all the prescription psychotic meds.

Those prescription drugs from her psychiatrist could cause birth defects. Although we wanted to eliminate the risk of birth defects, we knew that we would love our child anyway. No one can entirely eliminate the possibility of birth defects, but all we can do is hope and yearn for an entirely healthy baby. We spoke to her psychiatrist about what to do when and if Christy would become pregnant in the future.

The so called "shrink" told us that she'd just have to stop taking the anti-psychotic medications if she were to become pregnant. That didn't quite make sense to me. If she'd stop taking the anti-psychotic drugs then wouldn't she freak out, and go through a withdrawal stage? The doctor didn't have much of a valid answer for that question, but just told us in other words not to really worry about it. We just kinda left it at that, and didn't really pursue it much after that, but we should've seeked more opinions.

After Christy and I were dating for about a year and a half, I proposed to her, and she accepted without much hesitation. Her father was in town for Father's Day when I decided to do it. Her dad had dropped her off at my place for a while one morning before they we going to leave on a road trip to Tampa. Her dad told her that he would be back to get her in about an hour or so. My mom's parents were visiting that day, and they were preparing to depart.

After the salutations, I led Christy into my room. I went over to my dresser, opened the drawer, and pulled out a little white box. I said, "Baby I love you with all my heart, and would you do me the honor of accepting this engagement ring so I can spend the rest of my life proving it to you." She said, "Of course I will", and then I placed the ring on her finger and kissed her. She was wondering why I really insisted that we see each other before she left that morning. She surely found out.

We came out of my room and showed my mom and grandparents the diamond ring. We talked for awhile about the engagement. As the hour time allotment approached, we went outside to wait for her dad to come back. We waited for a few minutes, and then he arrived to pick her up. We hadn't talked much before this, but I just wanted to make sure to tell him that I had just asked his daughter's hand in marriage, so I did.

Christy gladly told her dad that she accepted. Then she showed him the sparkling diamond ring that I had gotten her. She got in the car, fastened her seat belt, I closed the door, and they drove away. They drove north from Cape Coral to Tampa. They boarded a plane to Dallas, TX once they got to Tampa.

As far as I know, her dad was glad about the engagement. I'm sure he had his worries, but he was supportive to my knowledge. I didn't feel like I ever really got the full story. It wasn't really all that important to me anyway.

Christine's father is an accountant for American Airlines which has its main office in Dallas, TX. He had recently transferred to American from bankrupted TWA where he had been employed for three decades. The visit that Christy had with her father lasted for a few weeks (maybe three). The whole time she was away we talked on the phone regularly.

The discussion about when we would officially have a wedding ceremony was always answered by me by saying that I needed to earn my college degree and acquire gainful employment first. There was no real date set, but we knew that we wanted to become married to each other. When we met, Christy was also in school, but after a while she just felt like she wasn't getting anywhere so she dropped out. By that I mean that because of her physical, mental, and emotional difficulties she just became unable to sustain herself academically.

I always encouraged Christy to try to stay in school, and sometimes I would try to help her study. She needed more of a full-time tutor though, and I was busy with my own schoolwork so I really couldn't be enough of a help to her. By the end of her college education, she was enrolled in a single class per semester which she wasn't able to attend on as regular of a basis as was required in order to actually learn the material. Her health just wasn't allowing her to live a normal life. So, she just decided to leave school behind, and concentrate on other, more pressing aspects of her wellbeing.

Shortly after Christine left school she did start feeling better in a way. The thing was that she use to tell me that she felt worthless. That really hurt me, and also confused me at the same time. I'd respond to her by saying: "you can't be worthless because your family as well as I and all your friends love you; you have a beautiful home, lots of money, and the ability to enjoy all of it". All of that just wasn't enough for her though. She was never quite able to get a sufficient amount of satisfaction from her possessions.

I tried to convince her that she was really lucky, and that there were many other people in the world who had a much worse time than she had. I never lived a day in her shoes though, so I guess that was easy for me to say. The way I saw her life was from the outside, and I also didn't have a bipolar personality disorder or her life history.

Following the announcement of our engagement the subject of a prenuptial agreement was presented to me. Christine's mother as well as Christine herself brought it to my attention. At first, I said that I'd prefer to sign one so no one would be in fear that I'm marrying her for her money. Then I spoke about the prenuptial agreement issue with some other people on my own, and then said to myself, "Wait a damn minute". I told Christy that I'd have to see exactly what the agreement says before I'll agree to sign anything.

Entering a marriage under the pretenses of a conventional prenuptial agreement pretty much is setting the marriage up for disaster. A marriage, to me, is when two separate people come together under the spirit of absolute love for one another to become one unit. A prenuptial agreement stipulates separateness of the two people who are entering the marriage. Marriage is not meant to be some kind of business contract; it's meant to be about compassion, sensitivity, protection, and respect for one another.

If we all could figure out what the basis for a strong marriage are made up of then the divorce rate wouldn't be so high. Both people in the marriage have to respect each other. Admiration would also be a positive requirement for marriage participants to possess.

The conservatives in this nation say that our society must protect the sanctity of marriage. That's a bunch of crap. If protecting the meaning of the union of marriage is the goal, then what needs to be done is not to prevent gays from getting married but calling for a concentrated effort to make sure that couples are compatible for the trials and tribulations of a marriage. With a divorce rate in this country well over 50%, it's pretty obvious that a lot of people out there don't know what they're doing when it comes to entering into a marriage.

Before a couple can obtain a marriage, license there should be a screening that they must pass. Repeating some customary words, and then saying, "I do" doesn't cut it anymore. So many other aspects of civilization have adopted innovative methods for doing things, and it's about time for marriage to get with the program.

All efforts should be made to protect the privacy of marriage because it definitely is a personal, family issue and not a business endeavor. A couple who is committed to each other and are able to show the dedication & respect for one another that is necessary for a lifetime of togetherness should be married. That would be protecting the sanctity of marriage while at the same time introducing a redefinition of marriage.

For some time while Christy was in school, and then for a while after she left, she was an independent beauty consultant for Mary Kay cosmetics. She'd sell cosmetics and other beauty products to interested people that she might come across in her everyday life through catalogues or her website. The problem was that she wasn't being very successful with it, and after some time went by, she decided to stop doing it. She'd have to place orders for products in certain amounts to keep her status with the company, and she wasn't selling enough to make a profit, so she was losing money doing it.

I really thought she loved doing what she was doing with her Mary Kay products though. Those were some of the best times of our relationship because she'd doll herself up, and just go out and represent. I felt like I was a part of the whole image too, so I'd try to make sure we portrayed ourselves well. The difference was that I was really happy at that time, but she must not have been.

She wasn't happy with herself. With the limitations of her cerebral palsy, the emotional scars of her past and present, her perceived need to be medicated (I don't mean self-medicated either), and her academic limitations, she just felt abnormal. I didn't let all those interferences stop me from treating her with respect and admiration, and to quantify our feelings for each other Enrique Iglesias's song "Hero" became our song.

When Christy and I spent time together we had limited means of transportation because neither of us had driver's licenses. In southwest Florida the main method of transportation for everyone is cars, trucks, vans, or SUV's so we were definitely uncommon in that regard. The majority of the time we utilized local taxi services to get around. Personally, my main method of transportation is the public transit system (the city bus), but Christy and I both preferred for her not to take the bus (especially not on her own). From time to time when we'd travel Christy, and I would get rides from family or friends.

Transportation costs for us became pretty expensive. I'd tell her that it's not much different than if we'd be bearing the costs of having a car. If we'd have a car then we'd have to pay to register it, monthly insurance, daily gas and/or tolls, weekly upkeep, occasional repairs, and a monthly car payment as well so taking taxi's is probably cheaper. On average we'd maybe be paying between $200 and $300 in taxi fares per month. The way I see it, having a driver's license is over- rated.

This past summer (2004), without even discussing it with me, she left me and the rest of her family in Florida to go up to see her dad and his family in Missouri. After she was gone for a few weeks, I decided that if she just was able to leave me like that for five consecutive weeks without much of a concern for me that maybe we should not be together. So, I called off the engagement. A few weeks later I got a package in the mail, and it was the engagement ring. I never wanted the ring back from her, and I thought she knew that.

Before she went to visit her dad Christy went to spend some time with her long-time close friend Wendy, Wendy's daughter, and Wendy's boyfriend. I'm sorry, but I didn't exactly trust that situation. While she was there, she was always doing something that seemed secretive or maybe something that I didn't think that an engaged young lady should be doing.

I broke the news to her while she was visiting Wendy. Before she left (the first day that she told me she was leaving), I said well don't expect me to be here to greet you with open arms when you get back. We had a pretty good argument that day which was really one of the only times we argued. I thought I made it apparent that I wasn't cool with her just up and deciding to leave town for over a month. She didn't care though. She left anyway.

After a few months went by, I was really missing her, so I decided to send her an email. After communicating over the internet for a while, she called me one night. We talked on the phone while she was visiting her dad and his family, but after a couple of weeks that came to an abrupt halt.

The phone conversations were going great for a while. We made sure to conclude each conversation by telling one another I love you and goodnight. We'd talk about all the things that were going on in each other's lives. One night she told me about a conversation with a psychic who told her that she'd write a book and gain celebrity status.

I said to her that I'd like to work on it with her when- ever she comes back to Florida.

She told me that she'd like that very much because she'd need my help to do it. She had a difficult time with getting her message out on paper to those who didn't know her. We were excited about the prospects for this endeavor.

Out of the blue she just said to me, "can you just forget about me". My response was: "is that what you want?" She replied, "Yes". I said OK and hung up the phone. I believe that was mid-September 2004.

By that time, she had been doing an intensive physical therapy program in Missouri while staying at her stepmother's home. Part of the program was doing Hyperbaric Treatment. Hyperbaric treatment is oxygen therapy that is supposed to help heal damaged bodily tissue. When Christine would tell me about it, she was quite excited, and very hopeful that it would take away her ailments.

Last November, at the beginning of the month, Christy came back to Ft. Myers, which I didn't find out until after Thanksgiving. On Thanksgiving Day, I spent time with my mom. Before dinner we were reminiscing about the past, and she mentioned that Christy had been with us last year for Thanksgiving; I said I'm not sure why she's not here this year too. The next day I decided to call her home phone number and leave a message.

I assumed that she was still up north with her dad and his family. Surprisingly she returned my call later that afternoon. We talked on the phone later that evening for an extended period of time, and she told me that she was sorry for saying what she had said to me the last time we spoke. She also said that she was mad at herself for treating me badly, and that she didn't know what was wrong with her. Telephone conversations continued for a couple more days, but then we decided to meet for lunch.

At lunch that day we each were in shock that we were back in each other's presence. We were surprised, and I can say for myself that I was really happy about the reunion. After we started eating our lunches, she told me that she had just had an argument with her mom. I asked what the argument had been about, and she told me that she told her mom that the two of us were talking again. Christy told me that her mom got very angry when she heard that.

My response was to ask if our relationship was our business. She said of course it is. I said, "Then we need to make the decisions about it and not your parent(s) or my parent(s). Our fathers didn't have much of a problem with us being together, but both of our mothers did.

We spent time together all through the month of December, and on New Year's Eve (which would have been our fourth anniversary), I asked her to accept back the engagement ring. Retrieving the engagement ring from my mother (who had been holding it for me ever since Christy gave it back to me a few months earlier) proved itself not to be an easy task. My mom's opposition to giving me back the ring was because she felt that Christy was holding me back from recognizing my full potential, which I saw as a bunch of bullshit.

On New Year's Eve we decided to go out for some pizza and then to a local comedy club. As we were eating our pizza was when I revealed the ring, and as I took it out and presented her with it, I guess she was able to know what was going through my mind because she asked me the question that I was having a hard time with. She asked me, "What does your mom think about us getting back together?" This was the first and last time that I wanted to lie to Christine.

The reason that I wanted to lie to her was because I didn't want to devastate her any farther than what she already was. Actually, I didn't want to devastate her at all; my intention had been to do just the opposite and offer her comfort from her torment. I feared that telling her the truth would destroy the effort I'd been making to convince her to be happy with herself.

I couldn't bring myself to do it through; I loved her too much to ever lie to her. I responded by saying that she's not too happy about it. She said, "That's not good enough, what do you mean?" To that I said that my mom doesn't want me to be with you because she feels like I can do better, and she feels like you're holding me back. Christy's response to that was to say, "That's pretty much true."

When Christy said that I told her that I don't care about my mom's opinion about our relationship, and baby you're always good enough for me. Then she held out her hand so I could put the ring back on her finger. When the ring was securely on her finger, I told her that I never want this ring back in my possession because it is yours forever just like my heart is. I thought we had agreed that night that our love for each other was all that mattered, but I guess I'll never know just how she felt about that.

A week and a day after we became reengaged, I woke up in my dorm room here at the university to a phone call from her mother. She calmly told me that it's not a good morning, and that Christine had passed away last night. The explanation that I got was that she took her own life by hanging herself. I thought to myself, "you fucking lying bitch". That was definitely not my lady's style (if she would have wanted to kill herself, she had an entire kitchen cabinet stocked with different medications which she could have and would have taken and died peacefully). She wouldn't have chosen to go out in one of the most painful ways to die that there is.

That day was the first day of the spring semester, and somehow, I was able to pull myself together to attend classes that afternoon. I was enrolled in four full semester, classroom courses for the spring, and one six-week, virtual (online) course. On January 10, I had three classes to attend starting at 12:30. After that first day of the semester I decided to drop out of my evening class but try to stay enrolled in the rest of them.

Not too long after the semester started, one of my roommates convinced me to look into the psychological counseling services offered here on campus. I started going to counseling which has been a good outlet for me to get things off my chest and hear feedback from someone who is trained to respond to situations of the type that I'm going through. I made it about halfway through the semester, but at that point, I had to drop another class. By the end of the semester, I passed two of my sixteen-week courses with a "C", and my six-week course with a "C" as well. I would have liked to have done better, but oh well (what can I do).

Christine and I never got to start working on our book with all of the other commotion that had to settle first. The way I look at it now after her death is that we're writing this one together. She's still inside of me along with my brother, and fortunately that can never be taken away from me.

Upon the passing of my brother, I planned to get a tattoo to honor his demise. For some reason I never actually went through with it. I guess it wasn't enough of a priority for me at the time. A few years earlier, a few days after I'd turned eighteen, Jason, one of his friends, and me all went down to the beach where I proceeded to get my first tattoo.

On the beach that day, I chose the design of a vicious, large, black cat. I thought the cat was a panther, but I've recently found out that it is a black leopard. The feline is on my left forearm portraying the image of climbing up my arm. I've been asked over the years why I chose that design, and I really don't know. It's a mystery.

After Christine's death I decided that I defiantly was getting a new tattoo. I decided to get gothic angel wings as a tribute. Under each of the wings I have initials engraved. The initials are: J.L.T.—for Jason Louis Tirado, and C.A.L.—for Christine Ann Loetel. The tattoo is engraved upon my right shoulder, and within the backgrounds of each set of initials is each of their favorite colors. The colors are yellow for Jason and purple for Christy.

Jason and Christine may have both been too innocent for this world. It's said that the innocent can't last. I've got to try to make some sense out of these two unnecessary deaths, and I imagine that the only explanation is that they were not meant for this life. They were destined for greater things. Although now, my philosophy of "no pain, no gain" has developed into "whatever doesn't kill me just makes me stronger".

8

SUSPICION

"A person starts to live when he can live outside himself."

—Albert Einstein

"No, this trick won't work...how on earth are you ever going to explain in terms of chemistry and physics so important a biological phenomenon as first love."

—Albert Einstein

"...one of the strongest motives that lead men to art and science is escape from everyday life with its painful crudity and hopeless dreariness, from the fetters of one's own ever shifting desires. A finely tempered nature longs to escape from the personal life into the world of objective perception and thought."

—Albert Einstein

How the hell was she capable of hanging herself to dea th?...

On our final night together, we went to see the sneak preview of "Coach Carter", and after the movie we went to a local sports café where the New York Jets were playing the San Diego Chargers. She told me that she would always be there for me, and I said that I only want you to be there for me morally. I told her that I didn't desire to acquire material things from her like everyone else she had known was very preconcerned with. By the time the football game was over she was pretty tired, so we just went back to her place and went to sleep.

Before we had gotten to the sports café, we were discussing the film that we had just seen. In particular, I vividly recall discussing the part of the movie that involved one of the female characters having an abortion. During our first year together Christine and I had an abortion which was a mutual decision on our parts, but in the movie the young lady makes the decision on her own. Neither of us was ready to be a parent, and we knew that abortion isn't intended to be a form of birth control, but at the time, considering the circumstances, we decided that it was necessary.

If Christy would have been adamantly opposed to the abortion, then I would have sucked it up and done what I had to do in order to be a family. She wanted us to be married before we had a baby, and so did I, but I know that in life we don't always get what we want, and I knew at the end it was really her decision to make. She didn't have much of a problem with getting an abortion though because she wanted both of us to be ready, and she knew we weren't.

Christine's mother was pleased to find out about the abortion. I'm not sure why, but the reasoning she gave Christy was to tell her that she wasn't physically equipped to go through a pregnancy or child labor. The other part of her objection to Christy having a baby was because of me (we were both disabled for God's sake). Any woman can pass on during childbirth, and that is an issue left up to the lady going through the birthing process and their God. No one else has the right to tell someone what to do in a situation like that; not even a mother.

The explanation that Christy told me was that she'd been told that it would be unfair for us to bring a child into the world. The child would be constantly ridiculed and would not get a fair chance to grow up as a normal boy or girl. With us both being disabled we wouldn't be able to properly provide for our child or give him or her a chance to live a conventional childhood. "Fuck all that bullshit".

With hindsight being what it is it may have really not been the right decision to have an abortion, put off marriage, or become intimate out of wedlock. Will any of us ever know the best way to carry on a significant other relationship? I guess that all we can do is hope that things will work out in the end and try to stay loving and compassionate to your counterpart.

Sometime after Christine had acquired her assets, a living will be drawn up to divide her estate upon her untimely death. I didn't expect anything from her to come to me, financially, but for the majority of her assets to be disbursed the way they have or will be is a damn injustice in itself (the original Will states what her mother instructed and not what she wanted). Her estate was kept in an irrevocable trust and was in the amount of roughly one million dollars when she passed away, which was all tied up in investment accounts through her bank.

Around a year and a half or so before Christine's death, the two of us went to speak to an attorney because she had some issues that she needed to be resolved regarding her trust and her Will. There were three parties who were trustees for her irrevocable trust, and they were: her attorney (who she felt was her mom's attorney and not hers), the bank, and her mother; she wanted to know how she would go about having her mom removed as a trustee. The conversation went on for about an hour or so that day with the attorney and his paralegal. She told me that she felt like her mom was too overpowering and she needed to break free from her. Christy also told me on multiple occasions that she desperately wanted to move out of her house which was across the street from where her mother lived.

When Christy was alive, she was under psychiatric care through a prominent psychiatrist in the area. I accompanied her to the doctor's office on a couple of occasions, and the impression that I got was that he wasn't telling her anything that I hadn't been telling her previously through my own common sense. The psychiatrist was prescribing medications for her though, and it may have been that I was unaware that the medications needed to be complimented with his office visits. I guess I didn't really consider that my level of what I thought of as common sense was not what was common for her. The combination of the pre- scribed drugs and the office visits were obviously extremely expensive.

Christine's mom definitely felt that the doctor was over prescribing her daughter, and that he was doing it so she would keep coming back to see him. About a year and a half prior to her death the doctor prescribed an anti-depressant that totally didn't agree with her. At that time, she called it quits between us, but that was after we had went out to a night club with my cousin, my roommate at the time, and another friend of mine, and she ended up drinking a bit too much and injuring herself on the dance floor. I thought that she'd be ok after a little bit, so we just ended up bringing her home to let her sleep it off. That sure didn't work out because she wasn't comfortable walking again for about a week.

After that night club incident, she was pretty mad at me for not staying with her while she was hurt. My reasoning was that I didn't know she was hurt that bad. Personally, if I take a spill like she did then I just would walk it off and forget about it. It didn't work that way for her because she was primarily off her feet for about a week. Anyway, shortly after she got better, she took a trip to Missouri with her mom and stepfather. Upon her arrival back to Ft. Myers we met for dinner. We talked about how we couldn't go on like that, and how the future would have to be different.

A couple of days later, during the evening time, is when Christy broke up with me. The next day I asked my roommate at the time to bring some things over to her house that I had over at my place. Having my roommate deliver whatever it was didn't turn out to be a good move on my part. I didn't realize that he would stick his nose where it didn't belong, but he sure did. Christy never admitted to me that anything of any significance happened between them, but my gut feeling was that something definitely did.

Some time had gone by after our break-up, but eventually we decided to go see a movie together. That was a difficult night. That night I ended up taking her to a local emergency room because she was psychologically freaking out. We ended up staying at the hospital until pretty early that morning, but we weren't done by far. They just told us to go to a local mental institution after talking to her psychiatrists on call person.

So, I brought her to the mental hospital, and we stayed there for a few hours while she got some things out verbally. When her regular psychiatrist's office opened, we went there and figured out what to do. They (Christy and her doctor) had previously been discussing a behavioral hospital about an hour and a half north of here that the doctor recommended that she should go to. We left the doctor's office and went back to her house, and she packed up some things grabbed her cats and left.

A big part of what brought out these issues in Christy was her relationship with her mother, and her mom's opposition to me. On our way to the behavioral hospital, we dropped off her two cats at a local animal hospital because Christy didn't want to leave the felines with her mom, and I wasn't allowed to have pets in my apartment. With the cats safe we left town and made our way up to Punta Gorda. We arrived in the afternoon, and upon arrival had to explain the situation fully in our own words. I'm sure that they had already been told (briefed) about Christy from her own doctor's office, but they needed to hear it directly from her.

She was admitted to the hospital, and after I knew that she was ok, my friend and I left. Her stay in the behavioral hospital lasted one week. During the week that she was there I made sure to call her every night. Christy did get to feeling better while she was in Punta Gorda, separated from her home situation, but after a week she was ready to come back home. She came back, and everyone tried to start over on a clean slate.

9

LET'S CHANGE-UP

"The further the spiritual evolution of mankind advances, the more certain it seems to me that the path of genuine religiosity does not lie through the fear of life, and the fear of death, and through blind faith, but through striving after rational knowledge."

—Albert Einstein

"We can't solve problems by using the same kind of thinking we used when we created them."

—Albert Einstein

"I've never let my schooling get in the way of my education."

—Mark Twain

"Peace cannot be kept by force. It can only be achieved by understanding."

—Albert Einstein

I am not a Southern Baptist Christian conservative, and I never can nor will be. My value is that religion is really only meant to control people while severely corrupting them without them being aware of it, which I am adamantly opposed to. One time when I was having a conversation with Christy, I asked her, if Chris- tians believe that heaven is such a great place, and they believe that all Christians are going to go there then why don't all Christians just kill themselves. We had that conversation about three and a half years ago, and she answered me by saying that God has a plan for each of us to complete. She went on to say, God doesn't want us to do that, and it's not up to us to decide when our time is up.

If someone were to pass me on the street today, they would get an impression of me that would make them somewhat uneasy. I walk with what is called a "drunken gate" so I always appear drunk or inebriated. If someone takes the time out of their busy schedule, and actually speaks to me then he/she will figure out certain things about me that probably would not have been expected. Really close-minded people would see me as some kind of criminal.

Now, and for the years subsequent to my car accident I've almost entirely taken on fights in an altered nonviolent sense. My current battles have been within myself and with society in general. At times I wonder why I even try to deal with all the corruption and idiotic bullshit in this world. I guess I've just gotta always make an attempt to stay optimistic. "Try to stay positive".

Maybe I am some kind of criminal (but probably not). Sometimes, in this screwed-up society, a person must sidestep the proper convention in order to get ahead (survive) or get the job done. Hopefully, the law will adapt to the changing needs of the population, and those who enforce it will not be so close-minded in the future. Maybe when or if that happens, legality can work more to the advantage of citizens, and not necessarily as a restricting mechanism. There are some people out there who definitely need to be restricted, but I see the law as being in need of many alterations.

Atheism is not what I advocate because I do believe in a supreme power. I guess I'm more of an agnostic, free spirit (definitely not an anarchist). The ways of the past can't continue to be the expected means for future existence because with the way that we, as society, are going, we're really going to be our own destruction. In our society there are many who are entirely too wealthy at the expense of the many low-class individuals who live in poverty, and I'm sorry to say, but that that is really fucked-up. If the mindset of just step on the poor guy keeps up then what's going to happen when all the poor guys are gone; it sure won't be utopia, but who wants that anyway.

Kill or be killed is kinda what our society is coming to. Are we all insane? Maybe I should just go out and stock up on artillery and go live in the mountains somewhere. Fuck that; how about we stop with all the violent hatred. In the past, we've had many people who have left great marks on society who have advocated nonviolent behavior (Ghandi, Martin Luther King, ect.), and I really think they had the right kind of ideas. These highly courageous soldiers are who really, I am inspired by and highly admirable of.

Malcolm X spoke of "whatever means necessary", but that would really be just feeding into the fucked-up spiral of hatred. The way to change the future is not to adopt the failed methods of the past. Wait a minute, violence has not always failed. Our country, the United States of America, has guaranteed its place in the world through much violence. It makes me wonder how we can expect our citizens not to be violent when violence has been the way of life for this country since the beginning of its history.

Damn, what a bunch of hypocrites if you ask me. "Practice what you preach", assholes, that's what I have to say.

Do the ends justify the means? I tend to think not, but sometimes I can agree that they do. Evildoers can try to justify their hateful actions, but their harmful intentions really are just proof of how screwed up in the head they are. Some- times I just say to myself, "what the fuck?" I guess my response to myself is "I live in a world of shit". At times if I try to have a happy mindset, I can be quite con- tent, but for the most part, when I'm around others I become pretty angry. They just fail to understand or even care about what they're really doing. That's cool because it's all good though, right?

What about our current presidential administration? They're more like corrupt businessmen than honorably presidential officeholders. I, for one don't want to see this planet eradicated by nuclear warfare. They tell me that the only way to fix problems like that is from the inside. Does that mean acquire their mindset? I hope not. Nuclear warfare isn't the only grave danger that our current political leadership presents us with, but it's probably the deadliest.

The Bush Administration in running this country like Ken Lay and Bernie Ebbers ran Enron and WorldCom, right down the tubes. Bernie Ebbers just was sentenced to twenty-five years in prison for his corrupt business practices. The trial of Ken Lay will be coming up soon. Martha Stewart was sentenced to jail time as well, but the severity of her crimes was not at the level of the Enron or WorldCom debacles, but I see the Bush Administration as being involved in worse crimes against humanity than even Enron or WorldCom.

We're also endangering ourselves by the way that we're treating our own environment. Daily, large portions of our living planet are being destroyed, and sooner or later the majority of the natural resources of our earth will be depleted. When that happens, we'll only have ourselves to blame (no, wait a minute, we'll all be gone by then, so it'll be our own future generations who'll have us to blame). We'd better adopt some new lifestyles in order to correct this problem before it's too late.

Spreading environmental education would, in my view, be a great start to correcting this catastrophic situation. Setting environmentally responsible examples would also be a big help to further the cause of environmental sustainability. Sustainability means meeting the needs of the present without compromising the ability of future generations to meet their own needs. I also recommend that our federal government and the Environmental Protection Agency (EPA) combine resources in a national effort to set certain standards for auto manufactures to only produce and sell low emission vehicles.

Efforts should also be made to phase-out the current pollution buckets that we have crowding our roadways. If this doesn't make sense to you then you should take the time out and really consider how much pollution the motor vehicle population is contributing to the destruction of our nature. The best way that I see to eventually eliminate the over polluting cars, trucks, vans, SUVs, buses, and large construction/transportation vehicles on the roads besides environmental education, and environmental leadership (which isn't coming along quickly enough) is by taxation.

Motor vehicles are a significant contributor to the pollution problem, but they sure aren't the only things that need correcting. All industry needs reworking in this area. There must be a universal effort calling on businesses to eradicate pollution as much as possible in the name of the continuation of the human race. Technology, like money, has the power to bury us all in its over excesses so let's go ahead and be courageous by using our intelligence wisely.

Having a vehicle and a driver's license are not rights, they are privileges. Having a driver's license and operating a vehicle should include the responsibility of being a socially responsible citizen. Unfortunately, we are still a far away from that point so now increasing the taxes on most vehicles that are on the roadway is the most valid option. When the time comes that we have a well informed and more competent public then this type of taxation can be averted. Hopefully one day the time will come when the human race won't live in societies that are utterly uninformed and seemingly unconcerned about issues of urgency (for example: environmental preservation).

The importance of receiving post-secondary (after high school) exposure to schooling is of such importance that we, as US citizens shouldn't have to be paying for it. Exposure to college level coursework is imperative for people to gain a complete understanding of their surroundings, and no one should be averted from it because of what it costs. The costs to society as a whole are much greater arising from an uninformed population so let's work to make this ambition of mine a reality. School also needs to evolve into a more inclusive, welcoming institution rather than a place for individuals of a certain mindset or those with mental abilities at certain levels. People who don't experience a full college education are really being deprived of the entire spectrum of what the essence of life really is.

What's going on here in our own country with our civil rights? For example, what's going on with the Patriot Act? Is it really intended for patriotic Americans or is it just an abuse of police power? An abuse of police power is what it looks like to me. We've not had another massive terrorist attack like the one on September 11, 2001, since then on America's homeland. I really hope no one thinks that the problem has been solved.

What about the wars that we're waging around the world? How many military people die on a daily basis? It's just a continuation of the same shit. Some people have told me that it's better for the terrorists to attack our military who are trained to deal with that kind of violence then for the terrorists to bring their war over to the United States. Do you really think that? Well, if you do then you aren't really paying attention.

By having our military forces stationed all around the world, especially in Muslim lands where they are extremely unwelcome, we are taking our war to their homeland. Who the hell do we think we are to do that if we can't deal with having citizens of other country's militaries here in the U.S? Wait a minute, they're already here, or are they? Let's just kill 'em all, and let God sort it out, right? No, that's not right. How about let's stop allowing our hey-ha government to keep us in fear, and stand up against injustices that aren't patriotically preservative, but wholly destructive.

George Bush thinks its right to inflict his values/morals on another country and its citizens who've not been exposed to a life in the lap of luxury like he has been. The Muslims of Iraq don't want democracy, and it's an illusion to think that we can make them accept it. Why does Mr. Bush assume that a democratic society in Iraq will work? I'll reveal why, because of his blurred perception due to a non-separation of church and state. Religious beliefs don't belong in the decision process for political issues.

That's real fucked-up to convince this country that it's necessary and patriotic to force another country to adopt a foreign way of life. Wait a minute that reminds me of what Christians do to non-Christians over here too. Are we going backwards in history here? We were supposed to have left that kind of thinking long ago. The founders of our country split from that kind of thinking in order to form the United States of America not so we could return to it hundreds of years later.

When our country fought wars in the past we were always engaged in the conflict for the betterment of our own country and to secure our own independence, right? Well, we need not to let President Bush convince us that this Iraq war is for our own good and will secure our independence. We're all adults, and we don't need the president of our country to tell us what's for our own good (like we're all a bunch of ignorant children).

The time has come when we all need to figure out that fighting these horrible wars is not the answer to solving global dilemmas. Evolution needs to move beyond recognizing gang violence on a nationwide scale as the way to deal with nations. Highly civilized individuals who have any intelligence should be able to look at war and be totally embarrassed by it. War is appalling and must be done away with in order for the human race to continue to thrive. For anyone who really thinks that our society is fine the way it is well all I've got to say is you've got another thing coming.

Nationwide healthcare, an end to homelessness and poverty, and increasing spending on fighting disease; those are a few things that are in the best interests of society to fight to overcome. Instead of squandering all those billions of dollars in Iraq on illusionary problems we should be spending responsibly on the very apparent scars of our own society. How about let's mind our own business while respecting other countries ways of life.

The Supreme Court shouldn't consider overturning Roe vs. Wade because people need to have a safe option for the termination of a pregnancy. A woman's right to choose what she wishes to do with her body is not the business of anyone but herself—it's a basic right, and that's the right to privacy which is guaranteed all over the United

States Constitution. For murder to occur there has to be mal- ice or aforethought, and that is not the case with abortion because its expensive, physically, and emotionally painful; besides that, a pregnancy can be the result of rape, incest or may kill the mother because of physical complications so abortion must remain an indefinite option.

I'm not saying I'm pro-abortion or that anyone else should be either, but I strongly oppose the government taking away this personal right of the citizens. Civil rights being decreased is backward thinking. The way to go on and prosper is to adopt forward thinking. Being pro-choice on this issue is essential to preserving the rights of society. Let's keep options on the table, and that way we can maintain a free society.

The justices of the Supreme Court should consider overturning the prohibition of alcohol. Yearly tens of billions of dollars are spent cleaning up alcohol related car crashes, and people's consumption of alcohol is among the leading causes of deaths in this country because of the anger, confusion, and violence it promotes not to mention the health complications. Cigarette smoking also serves as a great contributor to deaths and ailments in this country with huge financial costs as well and should be banned.

Marijuana consumption on the other hand serves beneficial purposes for individuals with any of an array of medical problems. The medicinal use of marijuana could and would actually be advantageous for society, but the fear of legalizing it must be that the non-medical use of the drug would be overly abused. At current times our legal system is somewhat indifferent to the use of highly dangerous drugs led by the likes of alcohol, all the anti-depressants & other psychological inhibitors that have been linked to countless deaths and suicides, and there is an innumerable amount of other prescription only drugs that are harmful as well.

So, what if marijuana was legalized. The stuff could be regulated for tax purposes, which would more than likely bring in more revenue than while it is illegal. Marijuana doesn't kill. The harm associated with marijuana is caused for one because it is illegal and for two because there are so many other destructive sub- stances that are being combined with it while it is sold illegally, on the street, that are causing the destructiveness associated with it. The dangerousness of the drug is minimal in comparison to many of the legal drugs available with a doctor's pre- scription. We have an association run by the federal government that is supposed to protect the citizens of this country from the abuses of harmful drugs that really isn't serving much benefit as of now.

My own brother is dead in part because of the ease of deadly prescription medications available on the streets of our neighborhoods. Deadly medications are legal and prescribed by doctors, and those prescriptions are converted into handleable drugs and sold as street drugs. Take deadly drugs off the streets by making them illegal, and let's focus our attentions on finding alternative means for alleviating illnesses.

The Food & Drug Administration (FDA) is not doing a very good job of keeping the public safe from abusive drugs, alcohol, or cigarette makers. If the FDA was really being responsible, then they would regulate these huge drug con- glomerates and big alcohol and tobacco companies out of business and have them find more beneficial ways of serving society.

Wait a minute; I think I've figured it out. The FDA is the fake regulator of legal crack houses that the federal government condones to operate as pharmacies. That sure is sad.

We claim to have a war on drugs in this country. Bullshit! You don't fight a war against something while at the same time condoning the very thing that you're fighting to eradicate. Come on people; pull your heads out of your asses.

The overindulgences that run rampant through this country really disgust me. I must admit though, I too, do take things that aren't necessary (my surroundings have made me accustomed to it), but I am making attempts to cut that shit out. I try to subscribe to the notion of the three R's: reduce, reuse, recycle, and I definitely would like to encourage others to do the same. To a great extent, this society gives much encouragement to backwards means for advancement and improvement. Why in the world are we rewarding individuals for being destructive and/or inconsiderate? I sincerely hope that I'm not the only one who this doesn't make sense to.

Not only does over consumption not make any sense; it is entirely detrimental to the existence of the human race. Societies really got to stop reading and believing about catastrophic destructions for our planet and get over their damn fears and start working for preservation. Pessimism—the feeling that things will turn out badly, is not going to get the job done. Let's prove that we are the most intelligent and most durable creatures that have ever inhabited this earth by simply preserving and not destroying our own environments.

The problem with the FDA is that it's in the pockets of the big drug providers (on their payroll, but not quite literally). Publicly traded drug companies, which provide prescription medications, have a responsibility to their shareholders to increase the value of their stock. They increase the value of their stock by driving up the demand for their drugs. Too bad that they don't really cure people, but just keep them sick, and needing their drugs because that's a damn travesty.

Back to the issue that I brought up earlier regarding the Immunization and Naturalization Service (INS), being ineffective. This country should have its population migration halted at its current level. In order to compose this war on terror successfully we must keep strict barriers on our borders, and uncover any plot being proposed by anyone already in our country. Let's keep the suicide bombers out of our nation, and perhaps we might want to consider modifying our own ways of life.

The INS should cease to exist, and all the people who are employed by it should be designated to fill new positions. Pulling the plug on the INS will be beneficial to all law-abiding citizens and will also help to protect our nation.

10

TRAPPED

"He who joyfully marches to music rank and file has already gained my contempt. He has been given a large brain by mistake, since for him the spinal cord would surely suffice. This disgrace to civilization should be done away with at once. Heroism on command, how violently I hate all this, how despicable and ignoble war is; I would rather be torn to shreds than be part of so base an action. It is my conviction that killing under the cloak of war is nothing but an act of murder."

—Albert Einstein

It wouldn't be the right thing to do to leave Iraq now that we've gone in there and done what we've done. Saddam Hussein and his government, while some in this country may have been extremely uneasy with it, ran Iraq functionally. That is what they want and need over there in that country in order to maintain stability. We don't need to have thousands of our brave servicemen and women get killed or be physically, mentally, or emotionally crippled for life because of a bullshit war or have upwards of 25,000 Iraqis get killed either. I bet lots of nations around the world are very much opposed to the ways that our presidents run our country, but does that give them the authority to declare war on the United States?

Hell no! No one in this country would stand for another country's military coming in and taking over. Well, that's what this whole fucking war is about. Our government can't even make good use of the oil revenue in Iraq, and we know there weren't any weapons of mass destruction there (they would have used them on American troops or the United States mainland by now), and there wasn't a direct connection with the September 11th terrorist attacks so all they have is hatred for Iraq's former way of life.

Money is widely known as the root of all evil, and which global nation has the most of it. Well, that's easy the U.S. does. I guess that we should have been included in George Bush's Axis of evil. Don't get me wrong, money can be a great thing, but it's really got to be handled the right way. I don't think anyone thinks that the Bush administration has handled financial matters properly, and I really think that they would be better off in prison.

The case for war made by the Bush administration in regard to Iraq was seriously flawed and untrue. In my book, and anyone else's with some common sense, that constitutes perjury. When diplomats falsify statements and documents to the general public, what has been done is called treason. Unfortunately, that is what has been happening in the United States and around the world for the last bunch of years.

Soon Saddam Hussein will be put on trial in the form of a military tribunal to face war crimes. The Bush administration should face charges as well for their lies and miscalculations leading up to the Iraq war, during major combat operations, and while their so-called reconstruction effort. Being held accountable works both ways.

We can't give Iraqis back their way of life because this war has made Iraq a recruiting ground for extremists and/or fundamentalists. Staying the course in Iraq will never accomplish our goal because no matter the number of bombers who kill themselves or our military kills, there'll be a bunch more ready to take their places. We've gotten ourselves involved in what's turned into a mess, and now we're damned if we do, and we're damned if we don't.

A quagmire is defined as a difficult situation from which it is hard to escape. That's exactly what we're involved in in Iraq. We would really be disgusting people to leave the Iraqi citizens to fend for themselves after the mess we've created, but if we stay there under Bush's Administration then we'll continue to keep spending billions of dollars and expending God knows how many American and international lives. Neither of those situations are something I approve of.

Let's learn from our mistake; not divulge deeper into it. We've got to make more of an effort to show Iraq and the rest of the world that we're only in Iraq to assist the Iraqis attain an adequate quality of life for themselves. Currently we're in Iraq imposing our will on them (installing a puppet government) using violent force. That's not the way to establish peace.

There is an insurgency in Iraq which is constantly growing. The country's infrastructure is gradually emerging, but unfortunately its progression is too slow, so it is another outlet for recruits into the insurgency. The insurgency must be dealt with like common street criminals being fought by police. It is not a job for the military. Definitely not ours.

We must make great efforts to uncover, decipher, and/or get to the bottom of the motivations surrounding the Iraq situation. In adopting that principle, the first thing I suggest we do is impeach our U.S.

president so we can solve this international predicament diplomatically; like it should have been taken care of originally. The reason that we must impeach our president is because he and his entire administration are cemented in the mindset that war with Iraq is the only way to solve this problem. On one hand I do feel that they are trying to solve this problem, but on the other I feel that our troops are over there simply for political/financial purposes.

I ask myself the question, as I imagine many other Americans do and have, has our presidential administration created this predicament in Iraq. Definitely not totally, but to an extent, we (the American people) sure have.

11

RESILIENCY

"Heroism on command, senseless violence, and all the other loathsome nonsense that goes by the name of patriotism—how passionately I hate them."

—Albert Einstein

"Gravitation is not responsible for people falling in love."

—Albert Einstein

"The most beautiful thing we can experience is the mysterious. It is the source of all true art and all science. He to whom this emotion is a stranger, who can no longer wonder and stand rapt in awe, is as good as dead: his eyes are closed."

—Albert Einstein

An unregimented extenuation of my education happened through the four years that I dated Christine Ann Loetel. Her mother's side of the family was and is Southern Baptist Christian. As I attended Edison Community College and after I was laid off from the Public Safety office, I regained employment as a student assistant for the mailroom. Her mother also worked at the college as a full-time employee in another department, which was near the mailroom.

While I worked in the mailroom I was always in the company of former military personnel, and always having war and other history as well as political discussions. My own ideas were refined by these conversations. Some of my current political outlook took shape during the two years of my employment in the mail- room at Edison College. Don't ever mistake my point of view as unpatriotic just because I don't agree with the president of my country (I never voted for him). Part of the duty of being an American citizen is expressing personal views for the world to see so society may advance from them.

These days multiple marriages are not that big of a deal, and that was reflected into my fragile fiancé. Fuck that, she wasn't fragile. If she would have been fragile then she wouldn't have been able to live through all that she'd been through with her struggles with CP. Christy had been opposed to multiple marriages, but at the same time she wanted to have a good, functional relationship with her mom.

Every time Christy would tell me that her mom was having a problem with our relationship, I'd tell her that it didn't matter to me, and it shouldn't matter to you either. I'd say c'mon Christy she's on her fifth marriage so she's no one to criticize our relationship. If she was any kind of an expert on marriage, then she wouldn't have been divorced so many times. I'd try to tell Christy that her mom's opinions need to be overlooked. Christine just wasn't really able to do that.

Her mother just needed everyone to believe that she was fragile, and they all did except for me. When Christy and I became involved with each other we were together pretty much always. Her mom thought that what was going on was some kind of rape. This was the furthest thing from rape that I've ever experienced. Not to say that I know anything about rape, but I do feel Kurt Cobain's *power ballad*, "Rape Me".

The unconditional connection that we shared was beyond compare seeing how we were both strickened with disabilities. Our home lives never coincided, but they never needed to. She had previously modeled, and I'm pretty sure that I could be seen along those lines as well. With her being labeled bipolar made for an extra difficult time. The combination of that with the CP (cerebral palsy) would have been enough for some people of weak standing to walk away.

Not me though, do you think I'm too dumb or too hardheaded? Dumb hard- headed fuckers like me make the world go round. One of my roommates seems to think that I'm some kind of crackpot, what a fucken moron. The other people that I go to school with and live with seem to totally not get it, I mean the way that I am. For example, this one fraternity on campus has tried to recruit me, but I simply want nothing to do with it. Maybe all these other students here want to become a bunch of corporate stooges, but not me.

In the end I look back on the time that we (Christy & I) spent together, and I really am grateful for it. Her death just hurts me so bad that I just want to lash out and go nuts. Some people have told me that they wouldn't be able to do the functional things that I've been doing for the last few months, but in a way, I have no other choice. The thing that I can't seem to prove is that I have a gut feeling that Christy's mom, Pam did this to Christy to get at me or simply because she didn't want her daughter marrying me. The cops won't look into that because just as she always does, Pam totally manipulated the situation and molded the outcome to her cold, calculating, experienced, and hateful liking.

Another likely reason for Pam committing this crime would be to send Christy to heaven. To me, heaven and hell are states of mind, and I feel that they coincide here on earth. In Pam's view, my outlook is very wrong because heaven is something totally different than life on earth, and so is hell (I'm not even sure if she believes in hell). She would have every reason to send Christy to heaven if it's really what she believes it is, but none of them would be her right.

Shortly after Christine's death I went over to Christy's house to meet with Pam and her husband. That evening we were discussing the death, and the main topic of conversation was the fact that Christy had stopped taking her medication about three months before she died. Christine's mom was adamant on blaming the death on Christine's father and stepmother trying to convince me that they were the one's who convinced Christy to stop taking her bipolar medication.

Now, I think I should tell you about Christy's mom, Pam. This woman is a real piece of work. She was employed as an assistant to an FBI or DEA attorney (I'm not quite sure which), for around thirty years. That was in Missouri. She's had four previous husbands, and now she's on her fifth. The control freak aspect of her personality would make me label her a megalomaniac. All those who encounter her are afraid of her, so she gets results. She's very manipulative.

In Pam's opinion and I'm sure she told Christy as such: we'd be married over her dead body. That statement speaks for itself, but I think it is usually only meant in a figurative sense. I believe here it ended up being meant quite literally, but in essence it ended up being over Christy's. On another account, Christy wanted to divorce her mother so she could become emancipated. That was some- thing she regularly mentioned to me.

Am I afraid of Pam? She can be pretty fucking intimidating. Maybe at times I am, but I can take care of myself for the most part. We still communicate some. Pam was out of work for a while, but she eventually went back which is understandable. Not for a woman who has no sense of compassion. She greatly misses her daughter, but she and the detective really botched the investigation, and what the fuck is that. It took nearly two weeks before I even spoke to the detective. I even had to initiate the conversation. Once again, what the fuck!

Fucking cowards, they all can go to hell and burn. When I finally spoke to detective Scott Thompson, I had to be the one to inform him about the molestation that Christy went through as a child from her uncle. What the fuck! Uncle Ed was the name that Christine hated. I also had to tell this guy that she couldn't hang herself (I had to tie the girl's shoes for her and cut her food for her). If any- one was totally in sync with her physical capabilities, it was me.

Christine confronted her attacker who raped her, and had her uncle locked up in prison for a total of eleven years. There was some kind of plea bargain agreement reached which to my knowledge is the only reason why this sex offender was released at all. A plea bargain is an agreement in a criminal case between a prosecutor and a defendant arrange to settle the case against the defendant. The defendant agrees to plead guilty in exchange for some concession from the prosecutor. The plea bargain was reached with the assistance of Christine's father who forgave his brother for raping his own daughter, and even went one step further to help him with his criminal defense (some sick shit).

After I told detective Thompson about the uncle, all he did was find out when he'd been released, where he was employed, and saw that there was no evidence that showed he'd left the state of Missouri. If that's all he needed to know in order to disregard the lead, then there is defiantly something wrong here. Chris- tine's uncle is a sexual predator, he's a criminal, and criminals know how to manipulate the legal system. While he was in prison he probably carefully, and methodically planned out how he would make Christine pay for where she'd put him.

My experiences with physical therapy, occupational therapy, speech therapy, and psychological counseling go on to this day. Do I hate the world I live in? Maybe I do. I'm not gonna commit suicide though. What'll that solve? I've been really livin' it up lately though (sex, drugs (whatever form that might come in), and rock n' roll). The problem is that it's kinda without reason.

Every day presents itself with a new kind of excitement for me. For example, today I have to take a written test at 12:30, but what new people and events will I encounter before and after that. Maybe I'll suffocate someone. Good thing that'll not leave any forensic evidence. How fucked up is that, people?

Does anyone see the connection yet? If not, then let me spell it out for you. When I left Christy on that Sunday (01-09-05), she went to go spend time with her mother and other family members for the afternoon. That afternoon was the first time that Christy was wearing the engagement ring in the presence of her mom since she'd been back. That evening when Christy left her mom's house, her mother escorted her back home because she had her own house. Everything I know about the situation leads me to believe that an argument started between the two of them about our marriage, and Pam's opposition to it.

I believe they continued to argue once Christine got into her house. The argument may have very well escalated into violence, and before Pam knew it, Christy may have been dead. Then the death may have been made to look like a suicide because for example: death by suffocation bears the same forensic evidence as suicide by hanging, but death by suffocation is murder. With around thirty years of experience with crime scenes and the laws of evidence she could have definitely altered the scene to fit into whatever her motive may have been.

This aspect of the situation was not ever even looked into because Pam had somehow convinced the officer that this was strictly a suicide, and it should just be left at that. What kind of detective is this, this guy can't even do his job properly. He needs to find new employment or somethin'.

Christine's mother did inform the detective about me. She told him that I don't need to be questioned because I am too disabled. She also told him that mine and Christy's relationship was not an issue because we had broken up months prior. This cop must have been real gullible or real corruptible. I believe that either of those instances would be grounds for dismissal.

Before Christy moved to Florida back in the late nineties, she had been dating a Southern Baptist Christian minister or pastor or whatever he is. Her mom didn't have a problem with that relationship, of course, but I guess Christy just didn't want to be with him. This former boyfriend of Christy's and friend of Pam was at Christy's funeral. Pam even had him speak about Christy, and she told me beforehand that I wouldn't be able to do any eulogy type speech (what the fuck is that?). That is another aspect of the death that I'm leery about.

Aren't the police supposed to look into all possibilities? If not her mother, then it may have been someone else. For these last few months, I haven't pursued this because I feel that I'll be putting my life in danger, and instead I've been writing this book. Once this book comes out the entire story will be laid out for all to see, and at that point, if someone wants to come after me because of what I know or what I've said then let them go for it.

Everything that I believe could just be things that I've blown out of proportion in my own mind. The thing is that I'm too educated to know that this whole situation hasn't been investigated properly; maybe it has and I've just not been informed. After being in the situation for over four years, I really was exposed to many of the inner workings of Christy's family that not really anyone but me could know or will speak about. I do and will though.

Now why in the hell would the cops not ever want to interview or even question me? Is it really because Christine's mother, Pam asked/told them not to? That sure doesn't make any damn sense.

Here's another situation that goes to the core of who Christy's mother really is. One evening Christy asked me to spend the night with her, and it was a Friday night, so I said sure. On my way over to her house I got a phone call from my dad, and he told me that he and my mom had had a fight and that he was thrown out of the house.

So, I spoke to Christy about the situation with my dad, and we decided to invite him over to stay the night in the den at Christy's house. My dad arrived at the house and shortly after just went to sleep. The next morning, we were all awakened very early by constant telephone calls as well as knocking on the front door. It was Christy's mom who simply became somewhat frantic about the situation.

I guess very soon after the phone calls and the door knocking started, my dad got dressed and left. Once my dad was gone Pam had Christy and I come into the dining area and sit at the table. She started by telling Christy and I that this would never happen again because of its highly inappropriateness. Then she proceeded to lecture us for a while along those same lines, but at the end she told me how much of a good shot she is. I ended the conversation by saying ok whatever you say Pam.

Later on, that morning, Christy and I left. We headed over to Cape Coral because Christy's house is in Ft. Myers. Before we went to lunch, we stopped by my mom's place which was where my dad was. He told us that Pam very nearly attacked him earlier that morning and had placed a homemade trespassing war- rant on the windshield of his car.

Christy heard that and immediately called her mom to see if her mom would confess to an attempted physical attack on my dad. Of course, she totally denied that anything of the sort ever happened. Hopefully, from that little scenario you can see just what Christine's mom was about.

My music really drives me, bands such as: Metallica, Godsmack, Korn, Mudvayne, Slipknot, Kid Rock, Linkin Park, System of a Down, Jay-Z, Tupac, and Eminem among many others are what I'm talking about. Sometimes I consider dropping out of school and divulging into drugs & crime. That would just be doing what the morons want, and I'm better than that. They say that music soothes the savage beast, but why does it have to be like that? Are we all a bunch of damn animals? I guess so. What's evolution anyway? Is it all just a hoax?

Fundamentalist Christians believe it is. They interpret the Bible literally, and disregard scientific discovery. Did God intend for us to observe the universe and test experimental notions in order to explain it or should we just believe some- one's distorted interpretation of what truths of the universe are. Better yet, maybe we should just believe some parts of the Christian Bible that suit us. The Bible is a work of fiction written by mortal men not by an all-knowing, all-powerful God.

I think I'm an addict, but who isn't. We're all just a bunch of pathetic addicts. Should we all just have a national self-righteous suicide day? We might be better off though, right. We'll be in a better place. Fuck that shit.

There are certain secrets to being closer to God, but there are many different interpretations for that. Jesus, Drugs, Sex, Music, Family, Homicide, Rape, and other forms of organized religion are some outlets that people may adopt. Do you know of others? Brutality is what our society has come to, and some would say that I'm pretty damn nuts, but I say I'm just a product of my environment. If you have any brains, you can see that.

12

QUALITY NOT
QU~~ANTI~~TY

(bigger isn't better)

"Any intelligent fool can make things bigger, more complex, and
more violent. It takes a touch of genius and a lot of courage to
move in the opposite direction."

—Albert Einstein

"Technological progress is like an axe in the hands of a
pathological criminal."

—Albert Einstein

Within my own mind I've never left Christy. I'm not saying I haven't indulged in things since her death. Just because she's not here physically doesn't mean that our spiritual connection has severed. At times though I find myself questioning her past faithfulness to me. Occasionally she'd tell me that I deserve better than her. Then again, I can see that she wasn't in complete control. Sometimes, I hate my ways.

I met someone a few weeks after my fiancé's death, and in my opinion, we really had some great times together. It only lasted for a couple of months, but I couldn't have really expected much more. I never really tried to compare her to Christy because Christy was way too unique. Although, this young lady was definitely on her own level too. In the end, after she broke up with me, I can say I guess I really don't blame her.

For awhile after we started talking, I didn't talk about my fiancé passing away just before we met. That was out of the ordinary because I can't seem to keep that to myself with anyone. I just got an entirely different feeling early on with her, and I guess I was going through a long-extinguished sense of infatuation. There did come a time when I revealed it to her, and she was ok with it at first. After contemplating my non-disclosure or whatever you want to call it, it became an issue in the relationship.

I've been told that it was just a rebound relationship. Maybe it was, but while it was going on I really thought I wanted it to work out. It's for the better that it didn't though because now I see that I definitely needed some time to myself to reconnect. At first, I figured that it wouldn't be a good thing to go around being totally depressed so I thought that having a new girlfriend was working to my advantage because I apparently wasn't depressed. I was really only fooling myself.

The recent death of my fiancé wasn't the only issue that caused the relation- ship to end, but she is a vegan, and I am not. A vegan is someone who doesn't consume animal products or consciously submit to the abuse of an animal either. She's a member of People for the Ethical Treatment of Animals (PETA), and I became somewhat consumed with that stuff too at least for awhile. She told me that she didn't want to be with someone who was being a vegan for her, but she wanted someone who chose the lifestyle. I just was not the person she was looking for.

The last time I talked to her we were still on somewhat of a friendly basis, but in the past with the girls that I've formally dated I haven't kept them in my life after we broke up. It's better for future relationships because keeping former lovers, no matter at what level, in the picture can cause problems in my opinion.

Where do I go from here? Starting up and continuing a conversation is no problem. The only thing is that I don't really follow through on things. One part of me wants to have a new girlfriend, but the other part of me would rather not bother for many reasons. It seems like every time I open my heart and make myself vulnerable, something shitty or fucked up happens to leave me broken and alone. I guess it's better to have loved and lost then never to have loved at all. Damn it.

Christy and I talked about how it must have been fate that brought us together. There were many events in each of our lives which could have led us to never meet each other, but they all happened and led us to each other with our greater understandings for mutual compatibility for one another. I feel that if fate brought us together then it must have been fate that brought us apart too. How can I fall in love with another when I was so much in love with her, and she left me in the way she did?

The other thing is that I really had a plan in my mind for what I wanted to do with myself for the next few years (graduate from college, start earning an adequate income, get married to Christy, have a baby, purchase a home, and start a family), but now that's all gone. I know I need to set new goals for myself, but it's easier said than done, and it's definitely going to take some time.

For now, I guess I'll just go on and see where the road will take me. From the death of my fiancé, I guess the lesson that I take away from it above all others is that we can try to rationalize relationships that we come across in our lives, but we've got to remember that the things we do can only go so far. Never expect to change someone, just love them for who they are if you choose to love them at all. I didn't try to change Christy; just tried to help her to progress (improve) so she would be able to make her life easier for herself. Was that trying to change her?

Through the life altering events of my brother's death, my fiancé's death and my own near-death experience in a car crash, I sure have had to utilize my power to adapt to alternate surroundings and circumstances. It seems that I can't escape certain things though, but that doesn't mean that I'm going to give up fighting. The world is just a crazy and mysterious place that certain people may think they fully understand, but no one really knows the complete truth and ever will.

13

UNEXPECTING

"My religion consists of a humble admiration of the illimitablesuperior spirit who reveals himself in the slight details we are able to perceive with our frail and feeble mind."

—Albert Einstein

The story of how Christy and I came to be together is worth mentioning. It was somewhat comical for me. I didn't approach her with the intention of developing a boyfriend/girlfriend relationship. I was reaching the final stretch of my relation- ship with Ondreya so I wasn't really ready for a new girlfriend.

An acquaintance of mine who I knew from vocational school was hanging out in the cafeteria at Edison Community College when I first started going to school at the school. We started talking to each other, and he pointed out one of the young ladies across the room. He told me something about how she wouldn't even talk to him which sparked my curiosity. So, I approached the young lady to ask her why she was ignoring this guy that I knew. She made it clear to me that she just didn't want to talk about it so that was that.

The next time that I saw her in the cafeteria I approached her again, and this time I did not ask anything about this acquaintance of mine, which she was much happier about. She was a nice girl and someone pretty easy for me to talk to. I found out later that from that second meeting of ours on she was attracted to me. We talked about all kinds of stuff, and she really liked my sense of humor. After almost two years she finally decided to give me her phone number without me ever asking.

I called her, but it was the wrong number. It took me a little while to track her down because I was kind of angry. When I found her, I asked why she gave me the wrong number. She told me that the acquaintance of mine who she didn't want to talk about had her number and kept calling her, so she had to get it changed. That had just happened, so she accidentally gave me the old number instead of the new one, but she apologized.

Of course, I accepted her apology (an innocent mistake). Soon enough I called her. We talked over the telephone during evening hours for a couple of weeks. On New Year's Eve of the year 2000-2001 she invited me over to spend time with her at her home. I just asked her where she lived and how to get there, and without hesitation I was there.

During our early conversations over the phone, I recall discussing my reluctance to enter into a serious relationship so soon after the difficult break-up of my last intimate relationship of significance. Christine asked me, "why is that?" My answer to that was to say that I guess I just don't want to make myself vulnerable to getting hurt like that again. She told me not to worry because she wasn't like that. I guess I didn't know what she meant so we just started to talk about some- thing else.

At this point, I reflect back on what she said to me that night, and I think I have a better understanding of what she meant. Even though her death ripped my heart out I know I have been better able to deal with it because of her. On the one hand I'm totally crushed, but on the other she taught me to have faith in love, so I believe she's living on within me. Her body may not be here physically, but her spirit and all the memories we shared together are right here.

That night that I first went over to her place to visit her I found out that her mom lived right across the street from where she had her own house. At that time, they had only been in the area for a few years. Christy and I turned on the original Rocky movie which we had both already seen. We pretty much just had the movie on for show because we had other things on our minds. After we were left to ourselves, we started to make out.

We ended up going "all the way" (making love a.k.a. having sex) that night. Early in the morning on New Year's Day (like 1 or 2 am), I ended up calling a taxi and going home. Before I went over to Christine's house that night I had dis- cussed with her my not trying to start any new serious relationship, and she seemed to be ok with that. My impression was that now we were just friends with benefits. I had even told her that I wanted a sex life, but I didn't necessarily think that a serious boyfriend/girlfriend relationship had to go along with it.

A description of Christy wouldn't be complete without describing her pets who she had a great devotion for. Her two cats were named:

Ray, and Belle. Belle was a female, light gray Himalayan who had a white underbelly, was very timid, and had beautiful long hair and piercing huge eyes. Ray was an obese calico who was very inconsiderate, clumsy, and at times rambunctious and violent with Belle. Lots of encouragement was coming to Christy attempting to persuade her to get rid of Ray, but she never would. She loved those cats like they were her kids.

The next weekend I went to a party at Jenny's (from Public Safety). At the party I ended up meeting one of Jenny's friends and getting her phone number. I don't remember the young lady's name, but we did go out the next night. We went out to play pool, she met my grandparents at my parent's house, and then we went back to my brother's place to watch a movie. We were in my brother's room on the bed with the door shut watching the movie **Wild Things**.

The mutual attraction was there, I had a condom in my pocket, but I just had something in my mind holding me back. It became late, and my brother and I just ended up taking her home. This was a pretty good-looking young lady too so after that night I was kinda mad at myself for not making a move on her. We continued to talk on the phone for a little while, but never ended up meeting again.

I did continue to see Christy though. In mid-February I met another girl at a bus stop who made it very clear that she was interested in me. I told this girl about my other situation that I had going on, and she told me that she didn't care. This girl was seventeen and I was twenty-one at the time and on top of that I wasn't really attracted to her. We did exchange phone numbers though.

That night she called me, and we gabbed for a while. For some reason, the next day I called her and invited her over. We met somewhere, and then I brought her back to my place. I knew that she wanted to do the "dirty dance" with me, so we went into my bedroom, but "gettin' it on" didn't work out because I just wasn't physically attracted to her. I attempted, but my equipment wasn't havin' it.

I ended up telling Christy about this seventeen-year-old girl that I had met. She asked me if I liked her. I said, "not really, but we did kinda have some sex." Then I found out that Christy and I weren't on the same page when it came to our situation. I didn't see or talk to Christy for about a month and a half after that.

When I finally caught up with Christy, I asked her why she was so mad at me. She didn't have much of an answer for me besides telling me to figure it out. I figured it out and I realized that I didn't want to lose her, so I came up with an explanation for what I'd done. I'd just try to explain myself by telling the truth and hoping that she'd listen.

The first hurdle of letting me explain was overcome with a little persistence. The explanation that I offered to Christine was that she never told me how she felt so I thought we were just havin' some fun as friends with benefits. She didn't know what that meant, but she hadn't mentioned that to me either. I said, "Well I'm sorry, and please give me another chance because I never meant to hurt you. I do want to be with you. Let me show you how much. I promise I'll be faithful to only you in the future."

Christine forgave me, and I never had a physical indiscretion for the rest of our relationship. I became very committed to her. Everything I did became for the best of the relationship and not for me anymore. I gave her much of my time and always tried to share financial obligations as close to equally as I could even though she had much more money than I did.

We each said, "I love you" for the first time after this carelessness had come about. In a way it worked out to make the relationship between Christine and I better. For the rest of our time together I took it upon myself to try to be a more developed (mature) person for Christy.

Before Christine moved to Florida, she had spent the first nineteen years of her life growing up in different places within the state of Missouri. After she died, we had a local funeral service for her, but following the service here in Florida her body was shipped back to Missouri to be buried. My request was to have her buried wearing the diamond engagement ring because I told her I never wanted it back, and I meant it. Her mother assured me that she was wearing it when she was placed into the ground.

I'd like to end here with a poem written by my mother about Christy. So here it is:

A sweet Angel in the Sky

No words to say goodbye

A shadow in the dust

No words will make it just

A young girl standing still

No words to give it will

A lonely lost life

No time left to be my wife

A big question is unknown

No answer why we are alone

A family across the way

No real reason to betray

A love to last forever....

No, I can't understand, no never....

Finished:

December 11, 2005

Andrew Tirado

AFTERWORD

The content of this book that was written in 2005, is something of a time capsule in my recovery that represents certain difficulties, regulars, and challenges. During the time of writing there I was obviously going through a bunch of stuff, but it's been largely exemplified that it's all stuff that we can navigate through effectively while staying functional. The degree that I graduated with from the College of Business at Florida Gulf Coast University is actually in the field of Management with a concentration in Entrepreneurship which is also known as small business management. Within Entrepreneurship is a subset of disciplines known as intellectual property. IP- Intellectual property has to do with innovation for things such as patents, copyrights, and/ or trademarks.

Patents are issued for inventions as well as certain improvements to existing products or services that are already on the market. Copyrights are issued for pieces of writing (short stories, biographies, and works of nonfiction, poetry, music, screenplays, and etcetera). Trademarks are issued for clothing lines, accessories, and/or other marketable namesakes. Other innovations may include alterations as well as new uses for or improvements to services or products that are already in use. For example, this book is an innovation to a copyrighted book that has been on the market since 2006, but I am the original author so I am legally able to do this update; it is also an innovation that the CRPS designation more or less came to and has been assisted with the publication of my book.

"Social entrepreneurship is an approach by individuals, groups, **start-up companies** or **entrepreneurs**, in which they develop, fund and implement solutions to social, cultural, or environmental issues.[1] This concept may be applied to a wide range of organizations, which vary in size, aims, and beliefs.[2] For-profit entrepreneurs typically measure performance using business metrics like **profit**, **revenues** and increases in **stock prices**. Social entrepreneurs, however, are either **non-profits**, or they blend for-profit goals with generating a positive "return to society". Therefore, they use different metrics. Social entrepreneurship typically attempts to further broad social, cultural and environmental goals often associated with the **voluntary sector**[3] in areas such as poverty alleviation, **health care** and **community development**." Quoted from WIKIPEDIA.com on 07-04-22.

As for this book, myself, and the pursuits of general health care, mental health care, and the plight of social entrepreneurship, I'd like to state that it's simply a work in progress. The effort to implement improved inputs & outcomes is at best messy yet noble, but as I've written back in 2005, that's just evolution. Looking back on these last sixteen years, some might state that it is pretty quincidental about certain aspects of mental health care advancement having become ingrained into many different aspects of our collective dealings, but others would state that there are no such things as quincidences. Back in 2005 & 2006, I didn't really have much of an idea that I was jotting down/typing up and engaging in everything else I was doing as my quest with social entrepreneurship. At the University my major was Management (as I've stated earlier), and I'd like to state now that the greatest objectives of management that I take away from the degree program are: time management, stress management, money management, social connection management, and knowledge management. This book, the certified recovery peer specialist label, and other things I do in the pursuit of better mental health care for others and myself are not the only innovative things that my involvement consists of; one mentionable thing is my online presence with email, Facebook, and YouTube along with lately Uber, but not really other social media.

When I began my professional quest my intention was not to help create, define/refine, nor activate/spread the goals of the certified recovery peer specialist profession , but I darn sure think I played some part in doing just that and for that I am proud. The CRPS designation with its four endorsements-adult, family, veteran, & youth, is primarily an emergency medical technician (EMT) type of specialized pursuit that is mainly funded and overseen by the department of children & families. Included among the roles of the CRPS is "change agent", and as part of that it is something that I've taken on to make more legitimized as well as widely regarded this profession. Mental health care and illness still aren't even regarded as human conditions that we all encounter to some degree on a regular basis by the largesse of society. That's why part of my vocation is to educate about the similarities and connections between physical health instances/occurrences/difficulties as well as mental health challenges.

In addition to the Certified Recovery Peer Specialist (CRPS) designation, I'd like to reveal that yes, it is similar to an emergency medical technician E.M.T. pursuit yet also similar to the pursuits of a social worker, but not fully removed from the work of an attorney or lawyer. I'd like to end this update by mentioning something related to forgiveness. We all can and will make mistakes, blunders, and/or miscalculations, but it is part of our human trait and task to rework while adapting to the changing conditions around us as well as within us. People, places or things can or cannot be with us for a reason, a season, or a lifetime.

"Nature is the source of all true knowledge. She has her own logic, her own laws, she has no effect without cause nor invention without necessity."

Leonardo da Vinci